THE HOUSE WITH ALL THE LIGHTS ON

THREE GENERATIONS, ONE ROOF, A LANGUAGE OF LIGHT

JESSICA LEIGH KIRKNESS

ALLEN&UNWIN

SYDNEY · MELBOURNE · AUCKLAND · LONDON

First published in 2023

Allen & Unwin
Cammeraygal Country
83 Alexander Street
Crows Nest NSW 2065
Australia
Phone: (61 2) 8425 0100
Email: info@allenandunwin.com
Web: www.allenandunwin.com

*Allen & Unwin acknowledges the Traditional Owners of the Country on which we
live and work. We pay our respects to all Aboriginal and Torres Strait Islander
Elders, past and present.*

 A catalogue record for this
book is available from the
National Library of Australia

ISBN 978 1 76106 907 9

Set in 11/18 pt Baskerville Classico by Bookhouse, Sydney
Printed and bound in Australia by the Opus Group

10 9 8 7 6 5 4 3 2 1

For Nanny and Grandpa.
May I find you here in all the days to come.

'It is well to remember that the entire population of the universe, with one trifling exception, is composed of others.'

—*John Andrew Holmes*

'It takes two people for deafness to be seen, one with hearing and one without.'

—*Nicolas Mirzoeff*

'Writing is simply the fossils of gestures, the traces left behind.'

—*Dirksen Bauman*

AUTHOR'S NOTE

In this book, you'll notice many variations of the word 'deaf'. Sometimes I use capitalised 'Deaf' to refer to members of the Deaf community or those who self-identify as part of a linguistic and cultural minority. This is a common convention in writing about deafness, and a strategy many Deaf people and scholars use to highlight cultural identity as distinct from physiological deafness. Others, however, don't associate themselves with cultural deafness and tend to use 'deaf' instead.

Though I largely use 'deaf' when referring to the audiological fact of deafness, I sometimes use 'd/Deaf' to highlight the dual nature of the audiological and sociological conditions. Where possible, I've tried to be consistent with this application. Though I'm aware that some reject the d/Deaf division because of the ways it might over-simplify highly complex sets of identities and cultural practices, I am adopting it here out of respect for the rich and vibrant Deaf community for whom it remains significant.

PROLOGUE

When I told my grandfather he was dying—translating the doctor's prognosis from English into sign language—he smiled and shrugged his shoulders. 'I've had a good, long life,' he said. With my hands, I explained that he was in multiple organ failure after a cardiac arrest, and that he'd been unconscious for several days. His condition was critical. Grandpa nodded, moving his gaze between me and the white-haired physician standing at his bedside. Once we were left alone, Grandpa took hold of my fingers and squeezed them tight. His face was calm, steady.

It made sense that I'd be the one to deliver this news. Having studied Auslan—Australian Sign Language—for a few years beforehand, my signing skills were the most developed and, with the exception of Nanny, Grandpa understood me best. My mum and Uncle Ray were drained both physically and emotionally after months of keeping vigil in various hospitals and eventually a nursing home. And my grandmother, being deaf too, couldn't have interpreted for him if she'd wanted to.

Grandpa had been sick for many years. His chronic emphysema meant he was often carted in and out of emergency departments.

Before his final stay in hospital, he could barely walk, and we pushed him around in a wheelchair Mum bought on eBay. On New Year's Day Grandpa woke up unable to breathe, and an ambulance was sent. He was monitored for heart troubles that weren't improving. We had five months with him after that. He never returned home.

In that last stretch, my family shared the load, organising between us that someone be present whenever possible to ensure that Grandpa had an advocate. Often, hospital staff had no clue how to interact with him despite the communication tips my mother plastered on the walls of each institution. 'Melvyn Hunt is DEAF,' her handwritten signs read. 'He cannot hear you even if you shout.' We grew tired of reminding people to get his attention before speaking, to look at him, or to use the pens and pads of paper we'd left so that he could understand and respond.

The combination of age and language barriers meant that his care was often compromised. Though Grandpa had excellent English, medical personnel could rarely understand his voice, and he struggled to follow the rapid-fire movements of their lips.

One night, early in his hospital stay, he had two blood transfusions without knowing what was going on. By the time I arrived in the morning he was wild with panic, vomiting blood and begging for answers. Nobody had explained what was wrong or why he'd needed the transfusions. He could only watch and wonder.

Having failed rehab by late March, he was sent to an aged-care facility, and in late April he was rushed back to emergency.

His death didn't blindside us. It was neither sudden nor unexpected. We had another three and half weeks with Grandpa after the heart attack, for some of which he was lucid and even joked with the nurses in the ward. All of us—Nanny, my parents, my siblings, my cousins, Uncle Ray and Auntie Ruth—watched on as he slipped in and out of consciousness, waking for occasional sips of lemonade and beer that we'd snuck onto the premises.

Those familiar with Deaf culture talk about the phenomenon of the 'long Deaf goodbye', where the ritual of farewelling one another tends to stretch on and on, far longer than in hearing interactions. Grandpa was unhurried in saying goodbye to his family. I like to think he was holding onto us just that little bit longer, savouring those last embraces and tidbits of conversation.

It has taken me many attempts to say goodbye. To me the process feels eternal—bottomless and unrelenting. Grief, as Joan Didion writes, 'has no distance. Grief comes in waves, paroxysms, sudden apprehensions that weaken the knees and blind the eyes and obliterate the dailiness of life.' Three years have passed since Grandpa died, and it has taken many such paroxysms to make any sense of the loss. There is no instrument to measure the mark a person leaves, no salve to remedy the ache. My grandfather's life was both ordinary and extraordinary—his deafness was so exquisitely misunderstood that every part of me felt summoned to translate.

1.

If I were to tell you our story in sign language—the story of my grandparents and me—I'd begin with a single finger touching my chest. My hands would form the signs for 'grew up' and then 'next door', a flattened palm rising from my torso to eye level, followed by my index finger hooked over my thumb and turned over at the wrist like a key in an ignition. I'd use the signs for 'my grandparents': a clenched fist over my heart, and the letter signs 'G, M, F' to represent 'grand-mother-father'. Then, placing two fingers over my right ear, I'd use the sign for 'deaf' to refer to them, and to describe myself, I'd use 'hearing': a single digit moved from beside the ear to rest below the mouth. I'd sign our closeness by interlocking my index fingers in the sign that doubles for 'link' or 'connection'. By puffing air from my lips, squinting my eyes slightly, and rocking my looped fingers back and forth, I'd place emphasis on the sign, the duration, direction and intensity of its delivery giving tone and shape to the meaning it makes.

Like the opening montage of a film, I would set up the space before my body, carving a visual representation of the dual-occupancy home where I lived beside Nanny and Grandpa for most of my life.

With my hands poised as though ready to play a piano, I'd sculpt a diagram of our long, narrow house, showing its shared roof and the single wall that separated my place from theirs. By turning my hands with the thumbs facing upwards, I'd slice through the air, two-thirds of the way through the structure, to mark out the four-bedroom residence that belonged to my parents, my sister, my brother and me. By repositioning my hands to the left and pointing to the remaining third, I'd show you the semi-detached granny flat where Nanny lives to this day.

In Auslan, stories unfold like moving pictures, with images sewn together in an art similar to cinematography. Narratives are rendered through a sequence of different frames, shots and angles conveyed by the signing body. A signer can zoom in or zoom out of aspects of the action by employing different visual and spatial tactics. Within seconds, a fluent signer might weave between a 'bird's-eye view', giving topographical information about the place depicted, and then, through shifting the body, will become the character in the scene as they open a door, for example, or rifle through a filing cabinet. Much like a panning or tracking shot, movement functions in these frames by directing the viewer's attention. Particular types of movement can also indicate shifts in character and point of view: where the body takes on a new set of idiosyncrasies including stance, gaze and range of facial expressions.

But I cannot write this book in Auslan. The language, with its own distinct grammar and syntax, has no written form. There is no accurate way to represent it on the page. Besides this, it's only in recent years I've known how to sign some of its parts at all. I am not a native signer. English is my first language, and dominant tongue. To tell our stories, I must write them down. I cannot do them justice any other way.

•

From the time I was little, Nanny and Grandpa were central figures in my life. They moved to Australia in 1990, the year after I was born. A part of me liked to imagine that their arrival in the country was linked with mine into the world, that I was the magnet responsible for having drawn them halfway across the globe. But of course, there were factors far beyond me. In quick succession, my mother and my Uncle Ray had decided to immigrate to Sydney from the UK. Mum left England after marrying my Australian father, and Ray came shortly afterwards with his new wife, Ruth. With both children gone, and new families forming, my grandparents soon followed.

Before we moved to the long, narrow house with the shared roof, my extended maternal family lived within walking distance of one another. If you look on a map you can draw a straight line that intersects each house: Nanny and Grandpa's place in the middle, Uncle Ray and Auntie Ruth's to one side, and my mum and dad's on the other. We'd get together every weekend for barbecues or curry nights, taking it in turns to host the gatherings. Sometimes I saw my cousins several times a week, when our grandparents would mind us while our parents went to work. We had our own set of toys in the playroom, with books and videos that were collected for our visits. The six of us kids often had sleepovers, cramming ourselves into the spare room where we screamed and squealed until the wee hours, unbeknown to Nanny and Grandpa who slept on soundly unless we made the mistake of turning a light on.

I was three when I first realised my grandparents were deaf. Before then, I'd sensed that they were somehow different from me, that there was a line that separated us. They didn't use the telephone; their doorbell had a flashing light and not a bell; and maybe Mum and Dad had told me that Nanny and Grandpa couldn't hear. But it was when I was three that I decided to experiment on my grandma.

She was stooped over the sink, washing the dishes. I stood behind her and screamed with all the force my little frame could muster. She didn't flinch. I howled, cried for help, thinking surely she'd respond to that. Nothing. In my indignation, my temper rose. I stomped on the ground, at which point Nanny turned around. 'I hate you,' I snarled, and watched as the colour drained from her face. I knew then that she hadn't heard me, but she'd understood. Afterwards, when I found my grandmother sobbing in the bedroom, I patted her hands and stroked her back, like Mum would do for me when I was sad. 'I'm sorry,' I mouthed, making sure this time that she'd seen my lips.

As a child I spent a lot of time in the company of Deaf people. Nanny and Grandpa's Deaf friends often dropped by for a chat and stayed for several hours. They spoiled and flattered me, pinched my cheeks affectionately. Whenever my grandparents held parties, I was drawn to the liveliness of signed conversations. Information was delivered with such verve and gusto, I wanted so badly to be involved. But mostly, I was an observer. To me, Auslan looked operatic and grand. There was something artful, perhaps even musical about its prosody.

It felt like an elaborate secret code that I could penetrate on occasion, but that otherwise remained obscure and unknown. The adults signed so quickly, while my skills were limited. I'd soon reach the inevitable juncture, the point where I could no longer follow or contribute to discussions. I would then gaze at the crowd before me, mesmerised by the uniqueness of individual signing styles. Everyone had their own flair and panache, their signature tone and energy. There were those who signed with utilitarian brevity, some were slower and drawling, and then there were others who possessed a cascading gestural intonation, with a seamlessness to the flow of their prose. Looking on as they chatted, I'd hum quietly to myself, composing accompanying soundtracks to the motion pictures before me: tunes that rose and fell with the dynamics of their movements. At other times I listened intently, enjoying the murmurs and sounds that punctuated Deaf interactions: the soft clicks and clacks of jaws, lips and teeth.

I loved the raw, breathy notes of my grandparents' vocalisations: the expulsions of air, the throaty gurgles of excitement and their raucous laughter that soared in pitch and volume. I liked to hear the swish of skin against skin as their hands brushed together in motion. Even the clunk of bone meeting bone, or the thump of a hand against a chest cavity felt to me like a kind of percussive refrain. When I was small, Nanny would often rock me to sleep while humming her own sort of lullaby. 'Tee tee tee,' she'd croon over and over on a single note. I'd doze off to the steady monotony of that repeated sound, and wake to the hushed, sibilant rasp of my grandfather's voice: the one he used when he signed to my grandma. As I'd stir, groggy and dazed on their couch, I'd see Grandpa's hands in rapid motion—a series of clipped 'shhs' and 'pahs' interspersed between his movements despite his efforts to be quiet.

Somewhere in the space between knowing and not knowing, in between these homes, and between Deaf and hearing cultures, I grew up. My mode of communicating with my grandparents was mixed, and sometimes fraught. Because Nanny and Grandpa attended oral schools for the deaf, where they were taught to speak and lipread in English, my family members relied heavily on their ability to follow spoken conversations. It was a point of pride for both of them that they use the dominant mode of the hearing world. It was easy, at times, to forget the drain on their energy that would follow extended periods of watching and deciphering lip patterns. But English was our default, and we used Auslan mainly for clarification purposes—for those instances where communication broke down.

Signing was by no means foreign. It was around me all the time. At home, our grandparents signed to one another, usually in their native British Sign Language or BSL, a close relative of Auslan. The two share an alphabet and many fundamental signs, but are different nonetheless. Signers between the two cultures can understand one another with ease. They're part of the British, Australian and New Zealand Sign Languages family (BANZSL), evolving over the years from the same parent language. Through their interactions with various Deaf clubs and groups, my grandparents adapted to the change, picking up new signs as they went along. But Grandpa continued to use his BSL numbers and would often query my use of Australian signs, particularly the ones I was taught by younger generations of Deaf adults.

With the very best of intentions, my mother sent my brother James and me to a bilingual preschool called 'Roberta Reid' in North Rocks. It had a combined deaf and hearing intake, and the two of us could fingerspell and use basic signs by the time we were three and a half. Because of a change in Mum's work schedule, my sister Lizzie never went there. She attended the local preschool instead. Nevertheless, all three of us knew to perform 'please' and 'thank you' when appropriate—Mum would insist on their use. She wanted us to have full access to our grandparents, to possess the skills and knowledge she had to scramble to acquire. Being immersed in the language, we picked it up quickly and easily. But as we transitioned into the mainstream, most of our skills fell into disuse. When I went to 'big school', nobody signed, and as English took over my days and my mind, I fell more in love with the shapes and sounds of spoken words. Signing was relegated to the periphery.

At Roberta Reid, many of my peers wore hearing aids throughout the day. These little devices were markers of our linguistic and sensory differences. My grandparents were never aided. They referred to themselves as 'stone deaf' and saw no need for amplification. But in the bottom drawer of Nanny's bedside table, us kids knew there was an old, neglected aid our grandmother had tried and hated many years earlier. Sometimes, we would secretly pull it out and admire it. Whenever we'd play dress-ups in Nanny and Grandpa's bedroom, we'd wait for Nanny to leave, and sneak a look at its waxy ear mould and taupe-coloured battery pack. Once, Grandpa caught me fossicking and bellowed. I thought I'd landed myself in big trouble, especially after it fell from my palm onto the carpet. But Grandpa seemed amused. Leading us to the living room, still swimming in their oversized clothing, we were each allowed a turn at adding it to our costumes. That afternoon I flounced around in my grandmother's floral dress, gesticulating wildly and running through the repertoire of signs I knew (yes, no, pig, chocolate, beautiful, cake, please, thank you), all the while with a plastic aid dangling precariously over my ear.

Some years later, towards the end of primary school, I can remember an Auslan interpreter visited and taught a group of us to sign the song 'I Am Australian'. It was around the time of the Sydney Olympics in 2000, and one of the songs in the opening ceremony, 'Under the Southern Skies', was performed, in part, in Auslan. As the woman engaged the class, I was bursting with pride. 'My grandparents are deaf!' I boasted. She paid me special attention then, calling upon me to share my knowledge with my peers.

But I could only tell them the sign for 'Australia', and maybe a few others. As she translated the song, verse by verse, I had an odd sense of recognition, as though long-dormant synapses were firing inside of me. The language was at once familiar and strange. Later on, I cried tears of frustration alone in the bathroom. I should have known those signs, and I didn't.

In the same year, when I was eleven years old, we moved to our current home, with Nanny and Grandpa next door. Located in Sydney's northwest, our house sits on a two-hectare semi-rural block, upon which we reared a few pet sheep, chickens, ducks and geese. In the mornings, Grandpa used to wander around the paddocks, leaning over the fences to feed the sheep their grain. Sometimes he had his video camera in tow to film the new lambs as they learned to walk. I'd often wake up to the shuffle of Nanny's slippers against the concrete outside my window, as she went to fetch the mail. Even with my eyes closed, I could tell the difference between their footsteps. Nanny had a quick trot: a staccato rhythm that reverberated through the cladding of the front verandah. Grandpa's was a much slower plod, often interrupted by heavy breathing.

By the time I finished school and started university, I shared breakfast with them daily. I'd trudge over in my pyjamas, and without fail, a cup of tea and toast was waiting on my arrival.

During our time living together, my mum developed guidelines for us to follow. Certain habits would grate and cause flare-ups of conflict. Often, Nanny and Grandpa would appear at our windows with their faces pressed to the glass. Sometimes they'd come around the back of the house and open one of the French doors, yelling out to get our attention. Mum would then emerge, red-faced and flustered by the intrusion. After one such occasion, Mum insisted on the use of our front doors. We were to ring one another's doorbells from then on.

The rules were made and relaxed, enforced and forgotten several times over. But always, Nanny and I formed a secret alliance—she encouraged me to flout the orders. Ringing the bell was far too formal, and so we devised our own way of announcing my presence. Instead of abruptly materialising in their lounge room, which often startled them both, I'd send our dog Turbo in first. I would open the sliding door at the back, letting him run inside, and wait until I heard them react. By the time I'd reach the living room, Nanny would be standing with her arms outstretched, ready to embrace me.

On the back deck, which runs across the length of the whole house, there used to be a lattice screen at the boundary of the two occupancies. Purple bougainvillea coiled itself around the slats of the wooden structure, creating a floral hedge. Nanny hated it and complained about the ways it obscured her view of what was going on. Several years later, when my parents decided to cement render the house, the barrier was torn down and never re-erected. Nanny was delighted. Nowadays, her washing line sits at the border, and, as she pegs out the clothes, she'll catch one of us reading or sunning ourselves outside and invite us in for tea.

On the bookshelves of our lounge room, my mum has collected almost every memoir and autobiography ever published on the topic of deafness. Though there's hardly a plethora of them in existence, the ones we had were always keenly read. My mother devoured them with a palpable urgency, scouring them for wisdom as if they were instruction manuals, or guides with which to make sense of her parents and the irreconcilable ways in which deafness is understood. Sometimes she dog-eared the pages when she came across sections that resonated. I always knew when she revisited them, because in quiet moments between us, she'd start to muse aloud. She'd probe for my opinions: why do you think Nanny does this? Or Grandpa does that?

Her appetite for knowledge is mirrored in her choice of career. For thirty years Mum worked at the Royal Institute for Deaf and Blind Children in Sydney. She was employed in various teaching roles during that time, with both deaf and blind pupils. For four years she was the principal of Thomas Pattison School for Deaf Children, and she spent seven years as the principal of Alice Betteridge School, a school for children with hearing and vision loss, along with other physical and intellectual disabilities. My mother is at heart an educator, and an eternal student. Both the books and her choice of work have been driven by an earnest resolve, and a dedicated service, fuelled by that doubled-edged affection and bewilderment with which we often regard the people we love. She studies and rereads, leaving her marks on the pages as part of that eternal quest that all children, to some extent, are bound up in: the quest to better understand and know where they came from, *who* they came from.

My mum often encouraged her father to write a book about his life. He was always a prolific reader with a mind and memory attuned to specific detail. In the past, when his reading habits were most ardent, Grandpa would turn his nose up at the latest depictions of deafness as tragedy or deficit, and Mum would suggest a challenge. 'Why don't you write something better?' she'd say. My grandfather flirted with the idea, but never quite committed to it. In later years she coaxed him further, fearing his knowledge would be lost and later forgotten if not recorded. Once, she brought over a pen and a pad of paper and told him to write everything down he could remember. But Grandpa never did, and eventually he said he was too old and weary for such an undertaking.

Around the same time, I began to write. I also enrolled myself in various Auslan courses at the Deaf Society of New South Wales, now known as Deaf Connect. As my hands discovered their 'voice', I found myself attempting to capture Nanny and Grandpa's on the page, embarking on the difficult task of translation and representation. Because I am my mother's daughter, my grandparents' stories felt like a kind of inheritance. My mother's yearning for insight, for understanding, is alive in me. I've dedicated the last decade to research in the field of Deaf and Disability Studies, writing academic theses, journal articles and think pieces on the subject of deafness and our cultural relationship to it. But because I am not my mother, I stand at a different vantage point. I have access to and distance from my grandparents that she might not. Perhaps I can navigate the space between our worlds, squeezing and shifting through the chasms, bridging the quiet gap between us.

2.

I haven't lived 'at home' since my mid-twenties. But like many millennial children, I've found myself boomeranging back to the family lodge from time to time—once after I returned from a stint overseas living in Amsterdam and London; another time after a breakup, and once more when I found myself writing a PhD and running out of funding. My siblings have been much the same, living abroad and returning many times over, Mum allowing our bedrooms to be left much as they were. In our adult lives, these moments of re-entry have sometimes overlapped, and we've folded into our old quarters, competing with one another for fridge space and time in the bathroom.

My sister, Lizzie, who is twenty months my junior, moved back home a few years ago with her two young daughters. Knowing his space would soon be invaded, my brother, James (who is two years younger than Liz), converted half of the garage into a bedroom and living area. His friends helped him gyprock the walls and place a floating floor.

Despite living a forty-five-minute drive away, I find myself drawn back there at least once a week. Whenever I visit from my apartment in the city, the house is cacophonous. Dad will be cooking dinner while my nieces scrabble on the floor with Turbo, the sound of children's TV programs left running in the background.

When they first moved in, you could find my nieces floating between the three residences: the main house, my brother's den, and 'The Cottage', the name Nanny gave to the granny flat. When permitted, they would tumble onto my brother's couch and play games on the PlayStation. In The Cottage, Grandpa would stream *Pinocchio* for my eldest niece while my younger niece toddled to the kitchen to ask for apple juice and Kit Kats from Nanny's pantry.

But even now Nanny and Grandpa's great-grandchildren struggle when using their bodies to communicate. Without the immersion we had as children, they've not quite mastered the strategies the rest of us have honed over decades. We remind them to move their fingers from their mouths and ask them to look at the person they're addressing.

In my family, stomping on the ground, pounding fists to a table-top, or flicking the lights on and off were all standard modes of communication. Our flapping hands and banging limbs were used as tools to flag Nanny and Grandpa's attention. Over the years, my cousins, siblings and I grew adept at manoeuvring to stand in our grandparents' line of sight. But if a back or a head was turned, we knew the value of vibrations and large sweeping motions.

There is etiquette to this kind of discourse. At dinner it's rude to flail your arms about, but perfectly acceptable to hammer the table. At close range, one shouldn't stomp, but instead reach over and gently touch Nanny or Grandpa's arm. From a young age, my family members understood the physicality of interaction. Transmissions started with the body. Words followed.

Us kids were recruited for communicative errands, the instruction: 'Tap Nanny' or 'Tap Grandpa'. As the eldest of their six grandchildren, I relished the responsibility, bounding over to rap my fingers against the shoulder of the intended recipient. Other times our parents acted as the intermediaries. If our hands were busy climbing or performing a special trick on the swing set, we'd scream the phrase until someone alerted our grandparents. When we had their attention, we'd mouth our instructions: 'Look at me!' we'd say, usually without voice, our little lips over-articulating the shapes of the words.

There has always been a kinetic element to the way we engaged with one another. I saw it magnified in differences between the two sides of my family. My father's kin delivered affection in dry pecks to the cheek and hurried, bony embraces. But on Mum's side, greetings were full and bosomy. Whenever she saw us, Nanny would launch herself in our direction, cupping our cheeks and smothering our foreheads with kisses. Her lips smacked against our skin in rapid succession; kisses were always delivered in a stream. When it was time to go home, she seemed to hold onto us forever, as though willing us to stay just a little bit longer.

We knew our grandfather by the feel of his woollen cardigans, and the sound of his playful grunts as we leaped at his chest to be lifted from the ground. At our request, Grandpa used to toss us into the pool at Uncle Ray and Auntie Ruth's house. He offered his body as a climbing frame and a source of amusement, letting us clamber onto his back for pony rides around the living room. He'd crawl on his hands and knees while his cargo clung to his neck or shirt collar. Our legs squeezed his sides and our fingers dug into him, but Grandpa paraded us round and round the carpet until he ran out of puff.

Whenever we grew tired of books and puzzles in the playroom, we'd come looking for Grandpa. We'd find him in his armchair, reading or watching telly, and pounce on his outstretched legs. If we climbed onto his lap, he'd recite the words to 'This Little Piggy', wiggling each of our toes and ending the verse with a burst of tickling. Sometimes we'd sit on his foot and, taking our hands in his, he'd bounce us up and down as though we were driving a horse and cart. When my niece was small enough to climb aboard, she would scale the length of his legs, throwing her head back in fits of laughter as he lifted her into the air.

Just as we manoeuvred to catch their eyes, there was a reper-toire of tricks our grandparents would use to seek us out. Grandpa would often address us with a big wave of his arm, clearing his throat as he performed the action. If he was feeling cheeky, he'd clap, stomp and bellow at once. He found our sudden reactions funny.

When Nanny wants my attention, she'll reach for me. It used to drive me mad—the incessant tapping until I looked up and met her gaze. Nanny forgets at times that I can look away as I listen. She'll pause mid-sentence if my eyes have wandered. She's sceptical about multi-tasking, too. If I'm in the middle of doing something and Nanny starts to talk, she expects me to abandon the task. If I carry on—even if I'm nodding in acknowledgement all the while—my grandmother will pause until she has my eye.

For her, the entire self is required for conversation. The only exception to the 'whole-self rule' is when I'm driving. Then, I'm permitted to keep my eyes on the road. If Nanny is in the back, she'll reach round the driver's seat to tap me on the arm. She'll deliver her message and then look to the rear-view mirror for my response. If she's in the passenger seat, Nanny likes it if I occasionally glance in her direction. She knows then that I'm listening, and even a micro-turn will elicit a pat to my thigh in acknowledgement.

For my grandparents, touch and sight were always interwoven. The very fabric of the world was experienced through the interplay of the eyes and the body. It was a currency us kids learned to trade in. We knew to duck and weave around signed exchanges; not to step in the way of hands in motion; never to enter the space between speaker and receiver. We knew, too, to be mindful of our lips and of the light. Standing in front of windows would cast shadows over our hands and faces. If the sun was behind us, we'd need to pivot, watching for our grandparents' signals, like the flicks of the wrist that told us to move, and the sign for 'perfect'— the thumb and index finger pressed into a circle while the others stand erect—when we'd found the right spot. At times we'd even catch ourselves tapping or waving in one another's faces, having slipped into that habituated mode of comportment we use in our grandparents' presence.

When I was a child, I realised quickly how to hold myself around my grandparents. The subtlest hint of impatience, disappointment or irritation could be detected a mile away. If I didn't light up upon eating, Nanny's brow would furrow. 'Don't you like the food?' she'd ask. If I was ever cranky or tired, Nanny seemed to know before I did. Grandpa too would accuse me of 'pulling a face' before I'd uttered a word of my anger. But Nanny was especially hawk-eyed, and it was hard to keep things from her.

In any space, my grandmother's eyes will dart around, taking in the spectacle before her. She enters a room neck first, as though pulled by the chin in the direction of unfolding action. Her chest and upper body are held erect while her head whips and swivels round. In open air, she's free to look where she pleases, but in confined areas, Nanny's gaze can be unnerving. While overhearing is discreet, overlooking is not. There have been times where I've sat with her in enclosed spaces and have watched as she admires the strangers before us. She'll pan up and down, taking them in, unaware—or perhaps unapologetic—that she's staring.

On occasions we're out together, Nanny might point at a passer-by. In sign language, pointing isn't rude. It's the way you distinguish between different subject positions: me, you, us, them. Still, I find myself shrinking away, wishing she'd put her bloody finger down.

But more often than not, my grandparents were the objects of other people's curiosity. My grandfather used to tell a story about a dinner they'd once had with a group of Deaf friends. They were out at a restaurant, signing to one another, when they felt themselves being watched. Grandpa described the gaping mouths and prying eyes. In response, the ten friends decided to turn around and direct the stare back where it came from.

'They didn't like that one bit,' Grandpa said. He always performed their reaction—body reeling, head jerking to the side to deflect the attention.

•

The Deaf Sensory Universe is driven by sight. The use of a visual–spatial language makes this so. Deaf people refer to themselves as the 'People of the Eye', a phrase first used by George Veditz in his presidential address to the National Association of the Deaf of the United States in 1910. It's a fitting way to describe the Deaf sensibility, where looking is tantamount to knowing. In Deaf circles, visuality is celebrated as part of 'Deaf Gain': the notion that there are unique cognitive, creative and cultural benefits arising from Deaf ways of being in the world.

When I first encountered the term Deaf Gain, sometime in my early twenties, it enabled me to see my grandparents anew. I began observing the gifts that come with sign language—communicating in noisy places, for example, or from across a room. With new clarity, I understood my grandparents to be 'hypervisual'.

Neurologist Oliver Sacks has written at length about the visuality of the deaf brain. Deaf people, he tells us, possess a superior acuity for analysing what happens in the peripheral visual field. The brain evolves as a result of experience, and the auditory parts of the brain become reallocated for vision. Though in the past deaf people were denied driver's licences, they are in fact the safest drivers on the road. They are more conscious of activity in the periphery than any hearing driver. The deaf brain, Sacks explains, is highly adaptive. 'Given a world of extreme visual attention, such as deaf people have, other parts of the brain are converted to visuality.'

Seeing provided a set of principles my grandparents lived by. For them, anything that could be seen was fair game for discussion. Nanny would often comment on how friends and family members were ageing or putting on weight. She'd pore over photos sent to her from England, and gasp over so-and-so's greying hair or bulging belly. If someone looked too thin, she'd suck in her lips and draw her pinkie finger down towards her navel. She'd diagnose issues with health and wellbeing almost entirely from the pictures, pointing to aspects of the image that supported her hypotheses. When my great-aunt fractured her hip a few years back and sent pictures during her recovery, my grandmother was concerned. Beryl was still in pain, she insisted. It was written all over her.

In the Deaf community, people are given sign names, which work a little like nicknames. They're used to identify people quickly and tend to reflect a distinguishing physical feature or aspect of personality.

These names are often visually striking. I know of one woman whose sign name resembles the sign for 'eyelashes'—four fingers of each hand extending up and outwards from the eyes. Another friend's name is performed on the forehead: an index finger drawn diagonally above his brow to reference the scar he acquired during childhood. Others are less flattering and might seem cruel. I know of one woman with the sign name for 'snot', because her nose used to run as a child, and another with the sign for 'breast' because she's busty.

Deaf people are known for this type of bluntness and, sometimes, their unfiltered commentary can unwittingly offend. As she was growing up, my mother found herself on the receiving end of the Deaf gaze. When Mum was a teenager, a deaf friend of my grandmother's visited the house. This particular woman hadn't seen Mum since she was a scrawny waif of a child, and as she sat on the lounge with Nanny, began to comment on my mother's changed physique. 'Julie's got fat!' she signed, rolling her hands into three distinct bulges; first at the face, then at the breasts and hips. As Mum entered the room, catching the end of the discussion, Nanny put a finger to her lips. 'Shh,' she said and waved the woman's hands down. My mother was crushed but never protested, knowing that visual judgements were just part of the Deaf way, one of those unspoken rules she didn't dare question.

·

Of all the distinctive quirks—the idiosyncrasies that marked my grandparents as deaf—none were more enduring than their preoccupation with faces. Nanny was always pushing hair off my cheeks. Hats and sunglasses, though she conceded their use in the Australian summer, were a nuisance that prevented full access to my facial expressions.

According to my grandmother, the mark of a good heart can be found on the face. Body language is observed and noted, but the face has primacy. It is the canvas upon which she reads sentiment, and by extension, an individual's character. Politicians, friends and even strangers are held to account over the shape and movement of their features. A former prime minister's crooked mouth and weasel eyes were enough to convince my grandma that he couldn't be trusted. By contrast, Peter, the home-help cleaner who visits once a fortnight, has a gentle, honest smile—a sign of his inner virtue.

If Nanny likes someone, she'll remark that they have a 'kind face'. When I ask her what she means, she struggles to tell me.

'I just know,' she says. 'You can see it.'

I remember once, after an argument between Mum and Nanny, my grandmother was devastated by the way my mother had scowled. Nanny paced around, raising her hands to her forehead. Hours later, when Mum returned to make peace, Nanny had forgotten the content of the discussion. She didn't mention the words exchanged but rocked in her chair with a far-off gaze. 'Your face,' she said, clutching her chest. 'The way you looked at me . . .'

Nanny's own face is round and moon-shaped with eyes that rove in search of connection. There's both a softness and openness to her features; her pillowy cheeks frame the arc of her childlike smile. Her ash-brown hair, which has only recently begun to grey, is always parted to one side, falling in loose waves around her ears. Each morning, she combs the wispier strands away from her forehead, and sprays them in place so that nothing interrupts her view.

When I was younger, I thought my grandfather resembled Dick Van Dyke. He had a mouthy, scallywag's face with a theatrical quality to its mannerisms: a firm jaw, long nose and wide grin. I loved to watch *Mary Poppins* or *Chitty Chitty Bang Bang*, imagining Grandpa was somehow connected with the movie. Both men were over six feet tall with gangly limbs, and there was something in Van Dyke's oafishness that felt familiar.

Grandpa would often teeter, and on those occasions his wobbly gait was transposed into physical humour. He'd recover with flair, brandishing his arms as though he'd staged a slapstick routine. As he grew older, his walking stick become a prop in his comedic gimmicks. But it was always the movements of his face that struck me most—the quick, clown-like contortions of mouth and cheek, the eyebrows that arched right into the forehead whenever a playful mood became him.

Many times, I'd leave Nanny and Grandpa's house with aching jowls, after giving my facial muscles a workout in their presence. Elsewhere it was polite to exercise physical restraint, but with my grandparents, deadpan expressions were not permissible.

Hearing people were often confounding for them. At times, spoken language felt inaccessible and wooden. Nanny struggled with 'mumblers', people whose lips barely moved. The local baker, whose shop was around the corner from Nanny and Grandpa's first Australian home, was a Chinese man. He didn't speak much English, and Nanny found it hard to understand him. Whenever we'd go to his shop to buy teacake, Nanny floundered. Even as a five-year-old, I was pushed towards the counter and she would ask me to order. As an adult I realised that the tonality of Chinese languages might have had a bearing on the man's facial movements, and thus on his engagement with my grandmother. But regardless, both he and the mumblers were indecipherable to Nanny. To her, they had monotone faces.

Because eye contact is crucial in Deaf culture, especially when signing, I was often conscious of the movements of my eyes. They told my grandparents much about my level of attention and affection. Turning away or breaking one's gaze is the equivalent of covering your ears in a spoken conversation. Looking was a form of respect but could also be weaponised. When I was little and Nanny or Grandpa would scold me, I'd actively avoid their eyes. Sometimes Nanny would attempt to lower my chin or twist my face towards her. 'Don't touch me!' I'd scream, recoiling from her hand. I often underestimated the power of that phrase: its potential to wound and generate rifts in its wake.

For all human beings, touch is a crucial part of non-verbal communication. As journalist Eleanor Morgan writes, 'The need for touch exists below the horizon of consciousness.' It is the first sense to develop in the womb and informs many of our social relationships. During the pandemic, Nanny was starved of touch. Covid made the world feel colder for everyone, but for my grandmother, social distancing had deeper implications. My family members refrained from hugging her for several months. Nanny complained and eventually pleaded with us. She didn't care if she got sick and said that a life without touch was barely worth living. Like many other deaf people, she struggled with masks, too. Without access to lips, she couldn't follow or participate in conversations.

I often wondered about my grandmother's sensitivity to touch. When I read about a study undertaken at the University of Oregon, my suspicions were confirmed: deaf people process touch differently from hearing people. Sight and touch, researchers have found, work together in the deaf brain, with auditory parts of the brain being used to process touch as well as vision. In an experiment, subjects were observed through MRI with an apparatus attached to their heads. These devices delivered flashes of light to the eye and soundless puffs of air to the cheek and brow.

The researchers adapted a known perceptual illusion called the 'auditory induced double flash' where a single flash of light coupled with two auditory events causes hearing people to perceive two bursts of light. Instead of sound, the puffs of air produced the same illusion in deaf people. The deaf participants were much more responsive to the tactile stimulation, seeing two flashes where hearing people saw one. The results showed the plasticity of the deaf brain, but more importantly, that deaf people actually feel touch in their auditory cortex.

In Auslan there's a sign called 'finish touch', which is used to describe past experience or familiarity with something. Someone might ask, 'Finish touch Spain?' or 'Finish touch China?' if they're enquiring about whether you've visited such places before. In English, we might say, 'Have you been to Spain?' Though the difference in translation is subtle, it's telling nonetheless. In the English sentence, the sensory experience is not assumed or prescribed in the question. 'Being' somewhere could take any form. But for Deaf people, touch is a synonym for experience. Being is always embodied, knowing is the stuff of flesh.

When I was growing up, I knew my family thought of language a little differently from those around us. Communication was always a knotted thing, and Nanny and Grandpa's deafness held a mirror to its instability. The first time I met another family like ours—one with deaf grandparents at the helm—was profound. After spending a few hours in their company, I noticed the overlaps in the ways we interacted. They tapped each other, banged on the table, and spoke without voice. A part of me exhaled and felt at ease.

But when it comes to accommodating deafness, family members are both the best and worst equipped. In hearing families with deaf members, it's an uncomfortable truth that few of us learn to sign. In our case it was only me and Mum, though Auntie Ruth once took a community course in Auslan, and everyone else could muster a few basic signs.

Over the years, my family developed idiosyncratic ways of speaking to Nanny and Grandpa, each of us with our own sort of visual 'accent'. If you were to watch us at a gathering, you'd see flicks of the tongue accentuated, harder 'bs' and 'ps'. There would be waving hands and animated faces thrown into movement.

My cousin Ben talks in a wide hiss, with toothy cat-like expressions and buoyant cheeks that bounce and contract as he goes along. My brother narrows his mouth, pushing air through rounded lips with slightly elongated vowel sounds. My cousin Emily uses no audible voice, excepting an occasional whisper that slips through her teeth. When she was little, Emily assumed all grandparents were deaf, and upon meeting her other set of grandparents in England for the first time, began to speak in the same silent voice she'd use with Nanny and Grandpa.

Between the six of us cousins, we've managed to acquire half-decent lipreading skills. Our movements and mannerisms are so familiar that we can follow one another's soundless conversations, watching for lip patterns rather than listening for words. But for the most part, sign language has remained foreign—part of our world but belonging to a different continent.

This isn't unusual in families with deaf members. Though 90 per cent of deaf babies are born to hearing families, only 10 per cent of those families will learn to sign. Most of my family can fingerspell, which is a way of manually representing English words with the fingers—especially the names of people, places or medical terminology. Though I've seen my father make attempts, he often does so with errors, and my sister and Uncle Ray never picked up the habit. Ray is dyslexic, and language of any kind provides obstacles. Even now, after years of Auslan classes, my comprehension of signs is much weaker than my production of them. Knowing this, my grandparents often spoke back to my signing, both as I was growing up and after I became an adult. It was a hard pattern to break.

However mindful my family may be, we're guilty of communication 'sins'. Any reputable guidelines for communicating with deaf people will tell you to avoid exaggerated speech or over-pronunciation. Such lip patterns can distort the shape and clarity of words. Despite this, the lot of us fall into the trap of troubleshooting with our mouths—convinced they hold the solution.

For all our proximity to Nanny and Grandpa, the members of my family have lived with different and deeply held truths about what it is to communicate. For us, our bodies were handy tools used as a supplement or precursor to language. For them, the body *was* language.

3.

At the front of my grandparents' house, on a panel of wood beside the door, is a Mountcastle Silent Bell. It's a visual doorbell system designed for members of the Deaf community. Connected to the main fuse box, it uses light to alert them to a caller at the door. As children, my cousins, siblings and I would clamber from the car and race to the doorstep to press that button. It wasn't enough to press it once, either. We would press that thing over and over until we heard the scuff of Nanny's slippers approaching.

Though no audible tune or chime is produced when pressed, there is a kind of musical quality to the mechanics of the thing— a rhythmic clicking sound upon each depression of the little white button. We all knew who was at the door based on the number of times the lights would flicker. If it was a single flash, it was a stranger; two or three sensible flashes, evenly spaced, and it was Mum or Auntie Ruth. If it was Uncle Ray, the lights would blink incessantly, a little gimmick that us kids found hilarious.

Nanny and Grandpa brought the bell with them when they moved from England. It was such a treasured possession that they carried it in their suitcases so it could be installed as soon as they arrived. In all their homes, both in the UK and Australia, they had electricians fit it to ensure that every room in the house was connected. Even the lights in the toilet were linked up to the system.

One of my favourite 'jobs' as a child was to 'turn the lights over', which meant marching to the front entranceway to flick a switch on a white box affixed to the wall. The phrase was my grandparents' way of referring to the day and night settings on the bell. Moving the lever to activate the day function would mean the electrical current could trigger the lights even when they weren't in use, and the night setting worked to save power (and ensure a good night's sleep) by operating only in the rooms where the lights were on. For years I watched my grandmother turn the switch. It was a crucial part of her daily routine, marking the beginning of each new day and the winding down of the evenings.

The bell was one of many assistive 'deaf-friendly' technologies my grandparents used daily. Their house was full of gadgets. Next to Nanny's bed was an alarm clock with a globe attached on top. It worked just the same as a regular alarm, only it made no sound, and the globe would illuminate when it was time to wake up.

For reasons I could never quite discern, their house was full of clocks. They were always the analogue variety and were hung on the walls of every room: the kitchen, the lounge room, and both bedrooms. There were four in the spare room, all in different shapes and sizes. Nanny had them propped on each bedside table and on the dresser beside the mirror. On nights I slept over, I'd collect them all and shove them in a drawer to stifle the constant, syncopated ticking. When my grandmother would come to wake me in the mornings, she'd quiz me over their disappearance, marvelling at the fact that they made such a racket.

Along with the clocks was a bevy of table lamps that sat among Nanny's angel figurines and blue and white china. They lived on top of the bookshelves and TV cabinet. Between Nanny and Grandpa's armchairs was a standard lamp with a wrought-iron base and a lampshade with a tasselled edge. It was my grandmother's favourite and always the first to be switched on at night. Of an evening the place was incandescent, washed in such a glow that the rooms felt warmed by a couple of degrees.

In our street, our house was known as 'the house with the dog in the window' because of Turbo's favourite perch on top of the couch, looking out to the road. But to me, it was the house with all the lights on.

·

In the study, on a desk overhung by photos of family, there was another luminous sphere that resembled a crystal ball. It sat beside my grandparents' fax machine and linked up with their TTY—a device that radically altered telecommunications for deaf people around the world.

A TTY, or a tele-text typewriter, is a boxy, digital device with a keyboard and a narrow strip of LED screen that can display typed text electronically. In the 1980s and '90s, before online chat rooms, Facebook and other social media, many deaf people used TTYs as their primary means of connecting with others, making appointments or social arrangements, chatting to friends or family members. You could communicate with anyone who owned a TTY, or alternatively, you could place calls using the National Relay Service, where an operator would receive the messages transmitted, and then speak them aloud for the benefit of the hearing person on the other end of the line.

The model my grandparents had was white with grey keys. It connected to the phone line through black rubber receiver pads that looked like Mickey Mouse ears on either side of the machine. Whenever a call came through, the spherical lamp would flash until the phone was answered, and the handset would be mounted and secured on top of the device. Once connected, you would type your greeting or ask who was calling, waiting for the answer to appear word by word in blue block-lettering on the screen before you.

In their first home in Australia, Nanny and Grandpa had the TTY set up in the study, which doubled as our playroom. Sometimes our games would be interrupted by the wail of an incoming call, and the lot of us would go charging down the hall, flagging Nanny down with our waving limbs before making the sign for 'telephone'—a thumb and pinkie finger splayed out and held to the ear and mouth. We knew that if Nanny was in the kitchen, she mightn't have seen the lamp going off. From the lounge and dining area it was clearly visible, but from the kitchen you'd have to lean over the breakfast bar in order to see it. Nanny would rush, flustered and exhilarated, in the direction of the study, and we'd crowd around and watch her in action.

When in use, the TTY made sounds similar to those you'd hear when connecting to early forms of dial-up internet—a squalling scramble of high-pitched peeps and whirrs. I often stood behind Nanny as she sat on a stool and carried out her conversations. Peering over her shoulder, I'd revel in the strange melody produced, and the patter of her fingers against the keys. Sometimes, in sillier moods, I'd entertain myself by putting on voices for each 'speaker', reading out the script as it lit up before us.

We had a TTY at home, as did Ray and Ruth. I used to jump at the opportunity to use it, and to show off my knowledge of how it worked. When I was in primary school, Nanny once sat with me and explained the speech conventions that dictated turn-taking in the conversation and even allowed me a go at replying to her friends on her behalf. At the end of each sentence, or when you were signalling to the other person to respond, you would write 'GA' at the end. 'GA' stood for 'go ahead' and 'SK' for 'stop keying'—an abbreviation that indicated the conversation coming to a close. When SK appeared on the screen, it was time to wrap up and say your goodbyes. The signal to hang up was 'SKSK': a final sign-off that punctuated the end of every call.

Whenever Nanny watched me at the machine, she would praise me and squeeze my arms when I remembered to press the appropriate keys. On occasions I couldn't respond fast enough, she never reprimanded me, but placed her hands over mine and typed to rectify the lag I'd created.

As I grew slightly older and more competent, Mum allowed me to make my own calls to Nanny and Grandpa, leaving me to chat away before bed, or after I'd finished my homework. By the time Nanny and Grandpa had moved into the house next door to us, TTYs were outmoded, and a computer soon occupied their desk. Instead of expensive calls to their friends in America and the UK, my grandparents could send emails instantly, and the TTY stood gathering dust, a relic from another time.

For a while, Nanny and Grandpa used fax too, mainly to contact Ray and Ruth who owned one for their plumbing business. On bits of A4 printing paper, they'd send handwritten notes back and forth, lingering at the desk to await a response. Sometimes my cousins would draw them pictures or write stories, faxing them through as gifts for their grandparents. When such creations arrived, they'd be displayed on the fridge for months.

There were other technologies too that were central to my grandparents' home. Though they lived off a small pension, they used whatever savings they had to buy the latest flat screen TVs, video cameras, VCRs and DVD players. Grandpa presided over them like they were precious artefacts that required expert handling. Every few years, Grandpa would buy the biggest television screen on the market, so the pictures and subtitles were clearer. Watching their TV was like reading a book with moving illustrations. Prose was delivered in fragments via closed captioning—transitions between camera frames like the turning of pages. It took me a while to absorb text and image at once, but my brain adapted over the years.

At Nanny and Grandpa's, I often watched television without the sound turned on. Something seemed to happen when the noise was switched off. Images seemed larger, grandiose, brighter somehow. I noticed lines and crevices in faces I wouldn't normally see. Without the drone and the din, the barrage of obnoxiously loud advertisements, I felt less screamed at. I could drop in or drop out at any time. By turning my head, I could avoid the insipid chatter of morning-show hosts. I could bypass the 'whodunnit' shows my grandparents loved and I loathed. My eyes provided escape routes where my ears did not.

Though I often sank into the quiet refuge of their company, my grandparents' home was otherwise a noisy place. Pots and pans were often clanged and banged, and I could always track Nanny and Grandpa's movements by listening for the sounds they made: the rattle of my grandfather's breath when he was concentrating on something; the whistle and sigh of the kettle as Nanny prepared tea in the kitchen; the clinking of cutlery taken from the drawer; the staccato beeps of the fridge when Nanny had left the door ajar.

Noises were a frequent topic of conversation. Nanny would see Turbo's ears prick up and ask what was afoot. Sometimes it was a possum clanging on the roof, or a cockatoo squawking outside the window. 'What do they sound like?' my grandmother would ask, and I'd fumble to put it into words. Planes would fly overhead, and Grandpa would remind me that once, years after he went deaf, he'd heard the roar of an engine. He couldn't be sure, and there was a chance it was just vibration, but the sound had registered in his ears.

Grandpa would comment too on our use of Discmans, iPods and iPhones, shaking his head as screens got smaller, and headphones became wireless. In the later years of their lives, Nanny and Grandpa were spurred on by their Gen Y grandchildren to purchase handheld devices of their own. When we bought them iPads, Grandpa spent hours trawling through Wikipedia and the online version of *The Express and Star*—the local paper from the West Midlands, where he'd lived in England.

When I moved out of the family home, I taught Nanny and Grandpa to use FaceTime so we could stay in regular contact. FaceTime, Skype and Messenger are all widely used in the Deaf community, and deaf users were early adopters of these platforms. Gill Valentine and Tracey Skelton have written about the ways these technologies have become an 'umbilical cord to the world' for the deaf. The video-call function has meant that real-time conversations can now take place in sign language, anywhere, anytime.

I looked forward to our FaceTime sessions almost as much as our visits in person. Nanny would set up the iPad on her little drinks trolley and wheel it in front of the lounge. Each time, my grandparents' faces appeared to me in a familiar frame—their heads suspended beneath a pair of my grandmother's cross-stitched pictures on the wall. Though they alternated between speaking and signing to me at home, our conversations online took place entirely in Auslan. It was a space they deemed safe and appropriate for sign. Perhaps they reasoned that a visual platform called for visual communication, the glimmering screen the medium for our exchanges.

Author Gerald Shea writes about the relationship between light and sign language, referring to the latter as the 'language of light'. 'The discourse of the Deaf,' he tells us, 'is not, as is the case of spoken languages, configured by the tongue and other organs of speech arranging molecules in the air, but by the motion of hands and other gestures that are transmitted by light to the eyes of their interlocutors.'

The deaf have long used light to innovate and adapt. In the nineteenth century, before Australian homes were wired for electricity, groups of deaf people would gather beneath lampposts of an evening to converse using sign. They'd huddle together, even in the freezing cold, to continue socialising into the night. This practice, which took place in streets throughout the country, is said to have led to the formation of Deaf organisations and clubs.

As a child, I often marvelled at my grandparents' sensitivity to light. On nights I slept in the spare room, the glow from my reading lamp would creep beneath my door and wake my grandmother. I tried reading under the sheets with a torch. This didn't work. Nanny would soon appear at my door and tell me to go to sleep. Even now, heavy curtains adorn the windows of Nanny's bedroom. The family home sits on a road with no streetlights, and still, the headlights of an occasional passing car can rouse her. For Nanny, there are no escape routes, even when her eyes are closed.

Darkness too, had a different weight and meaning for my grandparents. It meant the end of dialogues. There were no whispered words with the lights off before sleep. Blackouts, especially if there were few candles, were also a nuisance that resulted in early nights. Though Nanny insisted upon darkness while sleeping, there were times it also terrified her. It was a primal and inexorable fear. Without the light, her way of understanding the world disappeared.

My grandparents slept each night with a torch at their bedside, and at dusk my grandmother would close the blinds and draw the curtains. At five p.m., even if it was still bright outside, she would shut them pre-emptively. Nothing unsettled her more than people being able to see in when she couldn't see out. Equally, Nanny liked to see into each room in the house, and hated doors being closed. Us kids used to argue with her about it, disobeying her instructions and eventually bellyaching about privacy. For a time, we were in the habit of playing sock wrestling matches in the spare room, shutting the door to prevent her catching us in action. Sometimes she'd barge in, having figured what we were up to. 'No fight! No fight!' she'd screech. 'And *please*, don't close this door.'

Before I was born, my parents took Nanny and Grandpa to visit an underground mine in Silverton, just outside Broken Hill. It was a holiday my parents have recounted a few times, telling how they decided to take a tour of the disused shafts and tunnels. As the four of them entered the narrowness of the pitch black, Nanny began to scream and panic. She turned and ran back outside, back to the sun, where her senses could not betray her.

4.

My relationship with my grandparents has always been a dance between pride and shame. I swung between these poles much as they did—alternately wearing their difference on their sleeves or concealing it from the view of strangers. To me, their deafness was both a source of comfort and insecurity. For most of my life, I felt more at home in their 'cottage' than anywhere else.

As a child, I was painfully shy, especially around children outside of my family. I remember the first birthday party I attended in kindergarten almost as a trauma, with loud noises and raucous games. It was fairy themed, and my classmates turned up appropriately clad in tulle and glitter. My mum had given me a costume to wear and took my photo in front of the jasmine bush that trailed over our back fence. But the clamour of the occasion petrified me. While the other parents peeled away, I clung to my mother's leg and wouldn't move.

In the early years of primary school, I had one best friend who often invited me round for play dates. Our time together consisted mostly of reading our Baby-Sitters Club books side by side and swapping them over when we were done. I was often lonely at school, and on days my friend was sick, I went to the library and read by myself. In the time I spent alone, I watched other kids and the ways they'd play 'kiss and catch' or handball, swapping lunchbox treats between them. After careful observation, I tried aping them, asking Mum to buy Le Snaks and Space Food Sticks to trade. When she bought the no-name varieties, I was crushed, knowing I'd failed to gather acceptable playground currency.

Eventually my parents moved me to a much smaller school and were relieved to see me settle in a more intimate setting. Though my circle of peers began to expand and then deepen, what I craved most was the company of adults. I adored my teachers and longed for family holidays down the coast, less so to play with my cousins, but more to talk to the grownups. I loved to monopolise their attention, listening to stories and asking questions, especially with Nanny and Grandpa. In their company, I could chatter away without tiring.

Their home was a sanctuary, a place for old things and old souls. Being the eldest of the grandchildren, I was often the instigator and inventor of our childhood games. With the other kids, I dictated the rules and directed our play until everyone got fed up. Because there were only five months between Ben and Lizzie, and a month between Thomas and James, they frequently paired off, leaving me wanting a cousin of my own. Before Emily, the youngest of us, came along and I claimed near-exclusive rights to her, I'd often be left to play word games with Nanny and Grandpa. The three of us would sit in the kitchen with the contents of Upwords—a game similar to Scrabble—spread across the table. Other times I'd help Grandpa with his crosswords.

At bedtime, Nanny would come to check on me and find me dressed as my favourite characters from storybooks, silently acting out their parts while the others slept. Upon seeing me, Nanny would shake her head and smile. 'You're a funny wench,' she'd say, cupping the flesh of my cheeks and leading me back to bed.

Nanny explained to me that whenever she'd done something amusing or peculiar, her mother had called her by the same pet name. It was an affectionate moniker—one that Nanny passed down to me. To this day, she'll whisper it to me when I arrive at the house, squeezing my hand in hers.

As a teenager and well into my early twenties, I would splay myself and my books across Nanny and Grandpa's living room floor, stretched out in front of their twin reclining armchairs which sat like thrones overlooking the space. I loved the trinkets my grandmother kept on the buffet and in the cabinets—pieces of Wedgewood china in soft pinks and greens. My grandfather's bookshelves were full of classics and oddities. There were collections of poetry, sometimes written by deaf friends, many of which he'd hand me to take home and ponder. When I started a degree in English literature, I returned the favour, often leaving textbooks and novels lying around for his pleasure.

As a university student, I would retire to The Cottage after hours of lectures and notetaking, eager to see them and catch them up on my day. Nanny would have tea and lemon delicious puddings at the ready, laying them out on the patchwork table runners and placemats she'd made at her Deaf craft group. I felt keenly how differently my classmates spent their time, hanging out at the university bar and getting trashed on the weekends. I spent mine obsessing over upcoming essays or hanging out with my grandparents, sometimes with my offbeat friends present.

I thought my grandparents were brilliant. In some ways, I considered them superior to other people. They had been through things I could hardly fathom, and when my friends joined us for coffee, I relished the merging of my worlds. Within me, there was a naive, perhaps even childlike impulse to present Nanny and Grandpa to others, a declarative kind of 'show and tell' that oriented them to a vital part of me. These are my people. It's important to me that you know them.

But allowing others in could be complicated. When I was little, I used to forget to mention my grandparents' deafness. I'd invite a new classmate over, and invariably Nanny and Grandpa would appear on the back deck as we ran around the yard. I remember one time I was playing under the jacaranda tree with a new friend from school. We were scooping fallen petals from the grass and throwing them into the air like confetti, when I heard the back door slide open and click shut. There was Nanny, waving me over. Grandpa was leaning against the wooden rails of the deck, his upper body hanging over the balustrade. I bounded over to greet them, my companion trailing behind. As I began the introductions, I saw the look on my new friend's face. She eyed my grandparents warily, uncertain how to hold herself or respond when they spoke to her. When she didn't understand their speech, I translated for her benefit, and relayed her responses to Nanny and Grandpa.

Afterwards, when we returned to the site of our previous game, she spoke with urgency. 'What's wrong with them?' she asked, cocking her head to the side. 'Nothing,' I said, staring down at the grass. 'They're just deaf.'

I felt the sting of shame, of being 'other' by association, prickling through me in those moments. I feared that onlookers would catch sight of my own inner freakdom—the thing that made me different, more 'difficult' than others. There were layers of this feeling for both my grandparents and me.

Nanny and Grandpa were among the 30,000 Deaf Auslan users in Australia who identify as members of a cultural and linguistic minority group. Though they were part of a proud Deaf community, a group united by history, language and life experiences, their feelings about their identities were complex.

Hearing people are often surprised to learn that many deaf people reject the idea that they are disabled. Deafness is something they take pride in and is seen as an essential component of what makes them them. People who identify as culturally Deaf celebrate their deafness and prefer to use capitalised 'Deaf' to refer to themselves, while lowercase 'deaf' is used to refer to the audiological fact of deafness.

Terminology is important in Deaf circles. Preferences aren't uniform and using the wrong word can offend. 'Hard of hearing' is the term generally used for those who have acquired a hearing loss later in life. Generally, these people have a mild or moderate loss and prefer to communicate using speech, lipreading, and residual hearing. 'Hearing impaired' is often used interchangeably with 'hard of hearing' but is disliked by members of the signing community for its negative connotation of brokenness. 'Deaf and dumb' or 'deaf/mute' are highly inflammatory and are best left in the last century. And in health circles, especially in audiology, the term 'hearing loss' is widely used by professionals as a catch-all replacement for 'deafness'. A Deaf elder once described this to me as a 'hearing person's term'—a euphemism that sanitises and pussyfoots around itself. 'Deaf', he reminded me, is not a dirty word.

Though I never saw my grandparents refer to themselves as capital-D Deaf, they held themselves with all the requisite pride it entailed. They resented outmoded references to being 'deaf and dumb', particularly Grandpa who would rail about its suggestion of stupidity, and list Deaf achievements to anyone who would listen. Nanny was softer in her stance but no less proud. 'Oh, we're not radical,' Nanny would often say of their position. 'Deaf Pride' was valued but 'Deaf Power'—a phrase that mirrored the sentiments of the Black Panthers during the civil rights movement—was considered too harsh, too forceful, for my grandparents' taste. They were moderate and liked to think of themselves as such.

Grandpa would not suffer any suggestion that deaf people were 'less than'. He was particular about terminology and insisted on a modified version of the sign for 'deaf'. The standard sign, two fingers moved from the ear to rest below the mouth, was always an insult in his mind. He hated its connotations of muteness and dumbness, terms the Deaf community has battled for decades. Out of respect, I have always signed 'deaf' his way: two fingers placed on the ear.

My grandparents' pride was no small or ugly thing. But it ran in parallel, sometimes intertwined with their shame: a double helix coiled around a shared axis. I often caught my grandfather shrinking from the view of prying eyes. In public spaces, he'd bury his hands in his lap, hunch his shoulders and retreat into himself. In later years, when I started bringing boyfriends home, Nanny made a point of explaining that their deafness was a result of childhood illness. It became more pronounced as I approached what she saw as 'childbearing age'. Though many Deaf people locate their inherited deafness as part of an honoured lineage, Nanny was intent on reassuring my partners. She wanted them to know I wasn't damaged goods.

•

My father often told me I was 'too big for my boots'. It was an invective he used on occasions we found ourselves at loggerheads. I had a penchant for asking 'why?', a question my father found undermining. I once asked him why he always sat at the head of our table. What about us kids? Or Mum? It didn't seem fair. 'Because *I'm* the head of this family,' he barked, his chest puffing out as he cemented himself at his post. In my adolescence we argued over feminism, climate change and the faults of conservative governments. He accused me of idealism, I accused him of cynicism. But from all our exchanges, I gathered that I was too sensitive, too serious, altogether too much.

In my mid-twenties, when I read Susan Cain's *Quiet*, a book that makes a stunning case for the social value of introversion, I rejoiced. She explains the rise of the Extrovert Ideal (selves that are bold, gregarious and comfortable in the spotlight) and the ways that this has permeated our culture. 'The loudest have taken over,' she writes. 'Even if they have nothing to say.' On a personal level, *Quiet* was a balm. Introverts, Cain suggests, are aware that their temperament is socially undesirable and develop strategies to 'pass' as extroverted. She goes on to explain the link between introversion and the phenomenon of 'highly sensitive people': individuals who have more reactive nervous systems, who startle easily, and feel deeply. As I came across them, I read these passages aloud to my mother who confirmed I'd been that way since birth.

Though I was an old soul, I was also an anxious one. I worried about misunderstandings that arose in encounters between my grandparents and the hearing world. One of the curious things about loving a deaf person is the way you overhear and hold onto the taunts of others. The words of strangers have ricocheted in my head decades after being spat in my grandparents' direction. In the hot moments after such incidents, I'd fume and script elaborate retorts, detailing the shortcomings and ignorance of the offending interlocutor.

I never delivered such a rant, but sometimes I was surprised by the things that tumbled out, the ways that my shyness receded in my grandparents' defence. I remember one time in a supermarket when I was about eight, a middle-aged man asked Nanny to move as he tried to pass her in the vegetable section. When she failed to respond, he called her a 'fucking moron' and a 'bitch' and careened his trolley away from us, muttering as he went. Later, when we were paying at the counter, I looked up to see the same man behind us. He resumed his muttering and when Nanny made no response, he stepped towards her. 'Excuse me,' I said in my biggest voice, pushing my way between them, 'my grandma is profoundly deaf, and you are being *RUDE*.' The man fell silent, and we marched off.

My brother could be similarly defensive of their honour. In his early twenties, he was booking an Uber after a night out when the app let him know the driver was deaf. Upon seeing the notification, my brother's friend began imitating deaf voices, thinking he'd get a laugh. My brother, unsurprisingly, was not amused and slapped him in the face. The friend hadn't known about Nanny and Grandpa. They travelled home in silence.

In times of conflict, I often heard my mother's voice. 'You have to remember,' she would say, 'that most people have never met a deaf person before.' She knew acutely what it was to manage tensions in the air, to see new acquaintances regarding her parents as though there was something alien about them. Whenever Mum brought people home, she paid close attention to the subtleties of their behaviour, relieved when the newcomer approached conversations with warmth and openness, troubleshooting as miscommunications

46

arose. But there were the odd few who went rigid and recoiled at the foreignness of deaf voices. Bashfulness was understood but standoffishness wasn't tolerated. As far as my mum was concerned, such behaviour amounted to a moral failing.

My dad would often forget himself and end up on the sore end of my mother's judgement. On occasions he got frustrated by the stop-start motion of spoken conversations with Nanny and Grandpa, Mum would chide him: 'You could go deaf at any time, you know? Any of us could. And how would you like to be treated if that day comes?' Now that years have gone by, my father has significant hearing loss, probably from the grinders and machinery he works with in his shed down the back of the property. He often misses parts of conversations, and we find ourselves repeating them for him. No one mentions the irony.

•

In 2013, the Royal Institute for Deaf and Blind Children (RIDBC)—the organisation my mother worked for—released an advertisement that was plastered on bus stops and outdoor media spaces around Sydney, Melbourne and Brisbane. In the centre of the image was a teddy bear with no ears and no eyes. Above the bear was a caption: 'We need your help.'

I first saw the ad on a billboard in the city. I stood back, taking the thing in: the lonesome bear with its bowed head, the text made to look like cross-stitching that had frayed. Later that night, I brought a picture of it to my mother. Like me, she was horrified.

We sat together in the front room, gawping at the image in disbelief. The ad had been designed pro bono by an external company, with media space donated for the campaign. Nobody liked it, but neither the staff nor the Deaf or blind community had been consulted in the design process, and now it was too late. The bear was already out in the world. On the institute's webpage there was a statement explaining the ad was designed to 'stand out against the clutter of outdoor advertising' by using 'imagery that pulls on the heart strings'. The ad stood out, but for all the wrong reasons.

At the time, I was in the middle of my master's degree, writing a thesis about literary representations of deafness. I was reading and researching in the fields of Deaf and Disability Studies. I was incredulous that any organisation could approve of something so radically out of step with the people it served.

A few years prior, a woman named Dimity Dornan, founder and managing director of the Hear and Say Centre in Queensland—an organisation that provides speech therapy and audiological services to people with hearing loss—offended many in the Deaf community with her comments at the Telstra Business Women of the Year Awards. During her acceptance speech, she compared deafness to polio, calling it a 'scourge' which could soon be 'consigned to history'. People were outraged and Deaf Australia and its international counterpart, World Federation of the Deaf, made statements of condemnation and called for her to apologise.

Deaf scholar Breda Carty wrote about the incident, explaining how it might be difficult for the wider community to understand the claims that most Deaf commentators were making. 'They are proud to be deaf,' she wrote. 'They aren't interested in being cured; and they consider themselves to be a linguistic and cultural minority group.' On the night we sat staring at the bear, it felt like history repeating.

I wanted to write about it. Nobody had yet condemned the ad in a public way, and I wanted to expose it. Mum was uneasy about the idea, so I held off. Up until then, she had been unfailingly proud of RIDBC. Though she felt they had lost their way, she hoped they would restore their previously solid reputation. Soon after, complaints were lodged, and the ad was removed. The CEO issued an apology.

Still, I couldn't get the bear out of my head. Its eyeless, earless state was almost monstrous, grotesque. The reason it was horrific was the same reason it was effective. It preyed upon our deepest-held fears about the spectre of disability—lack, deficit, decay.

I had seen these fears reflected in the faces of others as they looked upon Nanny and Grandpa. The elephant in the room was more than a language barrier. To many minds, there was something abject about my grandparents' ways of being. The world beyond my family operated on a deficit model of deafness: one that understood it as a pathological condition. This was present in people who sighed and exclaimed, 'How sad!' when I mentioned my grandparents were deaf, or those that asked the perplexing 'would you rather be deaf or blind?' as though I had insider knowledge and could somehow help them decide on the lesser of two evils. I never knew how to negotiate these conversations and bit my lip or laughed nervously.

But I wasn't altogether immune. Though Nanny and Grandpa's deafness was familiar, many of the children my mother taught existed within the realm of the 'strange'. On a visit to Mum's work during the early years of primary school, I sat in on her classes and ate my lunch with her students. Many of them had multiple disabilities and required hands-on care. As I went to put some rubbish in the bin, one of Mum's students pinched my lunchbox and ate the remaining contents. I returned to find him licking the inside of my chip packet. I was furious and ran to tell my mother.

Imagining the boy would get in trouble, I dragged Mum to the site of the offence. When she erupted into laughter, admiring his ingenuity, I was appalled. I folded my arms and seethed. Sometimes I remember my scorn and feel chilled by it. Shame is heaped upon shame. But my mother's response was instructive. Without raising her voice, she acknowledged his cheeky manoeuvre, but she also celebrated the boy's nous. He had an intellectual disability, along with vision and hearing loss, and in that moment, she treated him with the dignity he deserved. I had wanted us to be treated the *same*. That day, I learned something about the distinction between equality and equity. Respect could be granted differently without it being unfair.

•

Inside of me, pride and shame were housed in separate but neighbouring compartments. Much as I tried to ignore this fact, they grazed against one another often enough to produce a kind of reckoning in my adulthood. In all the years I tended to the fault line between my grandparents and the world—the contact zones that carried the eternal threat of turning hostile—I'd never thought to acknowledge the feeling that accumulated like sludge in my belly. My strategy was to bury it. Deny it. If I could keep anything negative from Nanny and Grandpa, I would.

Sometimes, when cruel words were whispered behind hands and backs, I could get away with ignoring them. Unless someone's anger was direct, I needed only to interpret the bare minimum. I saw it as an act of saving face. Back then, I thought the bigger response was to rise above it.

But the layers of feeling—the residue of the unexpressed—began to tug at me. I threw myself at the problem the best way I knew. I began to read. From the university library, I sought everything I could from the fields of Deaf and Disability Studies: books, journal articles, online forums. I finished one postgraduate degree and began another, all in the name of excavating something I barely had language for.

In the pages of these articles, I found a kinship with scholars and activists that I'd never experienced before. Encountering the social and cultural models of disability was a philosophical 'A-ha' moment that radicalised previously starved parts of me. Unlike the medical model—a way of thinking that has dominated since the nineteenth century and locates a person with disability or deafness as a pathology requiring cure—the social model sees disability as a socially constructed phenomenon. In other words, society (rather than the impaired body) places limits on a disabled person. This doesn't deny the inequality or material reality of disability. Instead, it draws our attention to barriers in the social environment: the failure to provide accessible bathrooms or ramps, for example. It seeks changes from within the social environment to create access to the world at large. For Deaf lobbyists, this often relates to the provision of interpreters or the use of captioning in television programs to ensure equal access to information.

The cultural model, I found, has many overlaps with the social. It argues for accessibility but also recognises disability as a valuable form of human diversity. Some of these theorists write about unique ways of thinking that arise from cultural groups like the Deaf. 'Deaf Gain' and the benefits of deafness are often discussed in this vein, as is the idea of 'DeafSpace', a project that arose between Deaf Studies scholars and architects to outline a set of Deaf-focused design principles. I read about the 150 different principles identified in the study, which address five fundamental elements: space and proximity, sensory reach, mobility and proximity, light and colour, and acoustics. In essence, the principles are each intended to facilitate Deaf ways of communicating, such as broad hallways to accommodate signed conversation, a preference for open spaces to ensure visibility, careful use of light and colour to minimise eye-strain, and consideration of where and how sound resonates in the space.

In the months after discovering DeafSpace, I couldn't enter a building without analysing its accessibility. I noticed sharp angles, poky corridors and busy patterns. I began to look at everything differently.

Within this body of work, there were resonances with feminism and other social movements that appealed to me on a core level. Like sexism, racism or ageism, Deaf Studies scholars have a term to describe the prejudice experienced by the deaf: audism. Audism, as Dirksen Bauman explains, is 'a system of advantage based on hearing ability'. Others gave accounts of the 'Audist establishment', the various institutions, discourses and power relations that maintain the subordination of deaf people.

With singular focus, I ploughed through reams of relevant material. In Nanny and Grandpa's kitchen, I made notes about Deaf history while Grandpa hovered over my shoulder. One scholar, Aude de Saint-Loup, writes that the history of the deaf is 'a history of misunderstandings'. I learned that in ancient Greece, it was believed that anyone who would be a 'burden to society' should be put to death. In 365 BC Aristotle wrote that 'man cannot be a subject of instruction otherwise than through the ear'. As a result, it was believed that deaf people could not be educated, nor receive the word of God. Non-hearing, non-speaking people were presumed to be without souls and early religious accounts viewed deaf children as evidence of God's anger. Deaf people were considered savages, imbeciles, incapable of reason—no better than animals.

In more recent centuries, misguided philanthropy and paternalism has undercut much of the treatment of the deaf. The social Darwinism of the nineteenth and twentieth centuries saw that deaf people were encouraged not to marry or have children with one another. Eugenicists campaigned against the intermarriage of deaf people, and under Nazi rule, 17,000 deaf people were forcibly sterilised. Many underwent forced abortions, and an estimated 1600 deaf people were killed in concentration camps. Having been children in the 1940s, my grandparents were haunted by the Second World War. Nanny's primary school was bombed by the German Luftwaffe during the Birmingham Blitz and had to be rebuilt. It wasn't necessarily a targeted attack; many of the city's key buildings—the university, the art gallery, the cathedral and town hall—sustained significant damage during those years. But to Nanny it felt conspicuous, personal. My grandfather would immerse himself in documentaries that outlined atrocities committed by the Nazis, and Nanny used to remind me that Hitler would have wanted them dead, that if they had been born across the continent, he might have succeeded.

As my research continued, parts of a framework began coming to light, the scaffolding of a worldview that had previously lived in the shadows. These thinkers affirmed things I knew in my gut. They illuminated and clarified my world. Beyond the intellectual re-framing, a wounded part of myself came out of hiding, and I found myself reflecting on the clumsiness, however well-intentioned, of other lessons imparted by the world about deafness.

At school, I was taught about the five senses. My teacher organised a series of activities for my class, little experiments that would help us understand the ways that our bodies negotiated sight, smell, taste, touch and sound. To learn about taste, we had a picnic with all the different food groups represented at the table: salty chips, sweet jellybeans and bitter grapefruit placed on paper plates. When focusing on sight, half the class were blindfolded and led around the room by a partner who helped them navigate a path around the tables and chairs. Last of all, we were asked to imagine deafness, and were given orange industrial earmuffs and cotton wool to stuff into our ears. Alongside my peers, I sat in the semi-quiet, trying to complete the blank spaces in my worksheet. We had to speak to one another and write down whatever information we could grasp.

Afterwards, when the class discussed the exercises, my teacher said that our senses were gifts to be treasured, and that we should leave the room thinking about what it might mean to be deaf, or blind, or even to lose our sense of smell. Many of my classmates said how sad it would make them. But I went home feeling uneasy. I had never thought of Nanny and Grandpa as being without something. In fact, I never heard the words 'hearing loss' until I was an adult. Nanny and Grandpa were deaf. Until then, I had known that as a presence rather than an absence, a way of being rather than a lack.

Discovering Deaf epistemology—the unique knowledge Deaf people possess—was a breakthrough. It lifted a lid off a tightly screwed jar, allowing the opposing components of myself some air. But while it soothed, it also fortified. The problem, as Deaf Studies scholars pointed out, was political. Stories from the Deaf world were missing, routinely left out of mainstream culture. Deafness remained invisible in the cultural imaginary. In pondering visibility, I became fixated on our aversion to non-normative bodies. 'People don't like talking about, hearing or watching disability,' activist and wheelchair user George Taleporos says. 'It's not as sexy as gay rights or climate change.' Like George, I was familiar with this paradox.

Disability, and indeed deafness, is the thing we cannot look away from but cannot bear to face.

For most of us, our gender, race or sex, for example, give the illusion of being fixed: stable through time. But bodies, like identity categories, are inherently unstable. Disability or deafness can be acquired at any time. The existential stakes are high, and nobody dares utter the heart of that fear: that without sight or sound, or the use of our limbs, one's humanity might also be on the line.

Deafness might be the most interior of 'disabilities'. Unless a cochlear implant or hearing aid is worn and plain to see, there is nothing to mark the separateness of that individual. Until a person begins to speak or sign, their difference is undetectable. Nanny always despaired about this fact. It led to such confusion, such misunderstanding. There were other misunderstandings that Grandpa used to point out. He once remarked upon the incessant, almost compulsive use of the word 'silent' in descriptions of the Deaf world. Most of the books we owned on deafness had 'silent' in their titles. For most hearing people, silence represents melancholy and absence. Silence is exile. Silence is death. But for deaf people who have never heard, there is no absence to contend with. And for those who retain some residual hearing, silence is an inaccurate descriptor of their sensory experience. Sound is received in the body in all sorts of ways.

Deafness disrupts, disorients hearing ways of knowing the world. It is a reminder, both of our difference and our sameness.

Within the hearing world, there's an expectation that when we speak, we will be understood. The English language contains a whole host of aural metaphors for this phenomenon: 'being heard', 'being listened to', 'lending an ear', 'hearing someone out'. In the

Deaf community there is no such assumption. Deaf people routinely expect—at least in hearing company—to be misunderstood.

Inside the Deaf world, there is no language barrier to navigate. But in interactions between the deaf and the hearing, communication is a process of trial and error, and the onus is always on the deaf person. In an effort to be understood, I've seen Deaf friends mime, offer iPads as visual aids or type messages back and forth on their phones. They know to adapt and accommodate the other person. It's a skill, but it's also the generosity that takes me aback, especially given the fact that while hearing people can learn to sign, deaf people cannot learn to hear.

In the years I've navigated its light and shade, it remains true that from within the Deaf community, Nanny and Grandpa had no disability to manage. Among their peers, their language and their sensibility were never under threat. It is hard to escape the fact that in large groups of hearing people—including our family—Nanny and Grandpa were left out of a lot. No matter how we tried to include them, they ended up isolated. The bigger the group, the more they missed. And the more likely they were to be met with 'never mind' or 'it's nothing'—the dreaded phrases we offered up as excuses when conversations ran quick or dense.

It's equally true that, from within The Cottage, in uninterrupted moments, when the three of us sat with cups and tea and the noiseless TV in the background, I experienced a peace I cannot recreate elsewhere. In my grandparents' presence, parts of me—the most inward and precious—came to rest in the quiet.

5.

For as long as I can remember, Grandpa's eye seemed permanently attached to the viewfinder of his most prized possession: a black Sony camcorder. The device was one of many gadgets that I was forbidden to touch. The TV, DVD player, computer and his iPad all fell under his jurisdiction alone. But it was the handheld video camera that I remember as an extension of my grandfather's long-limbed frame.

Grandpa filmed everything. He filmed our birthday parties, family functions, school presentations and dances. He filmed parades and street festivals and had a penchant for videoing trains and ships. In his home collection there were reels and reels of footage, later converted to DVD, that documented almost every incoming cruise liner to Sydney Harbour in the 1990s.

His archives were organised with clerical precision. A table of contents lined the insides of each DVD case. My grandfather's fastidiousness in this domain gave us easy passage to our shared past. As someone who habitually documents life events through photographs, mementos or journaling, I understood Grandpa's impulse. But much of the material he captured—the hours of tape with no discernible narrative—remains mystifying both to me and my family members.

Grandpa once filmed a convoy of ants carrying a crumb of food back to their nest. He hooked the camera up to the TV to show my siblings and me. Upon our viewing, my dad sneered in the background, away from Grandpa's view: 'What the hell is he filming this shit for?'

I knew from a young age that my grandfather saw things in a way that I did not. His compulsion to record even the smallest, most insignificant things felt like a kind of cataloguing—capturing little marvels for safekeeping.

Before his love of making films emerged, Grandpa had long been a cinephile. When he was a boy, he used to attend the cinema up to three times a week. He would arrive at lunchtime and sneak in halfway through a screening, staying until the reel began again. Back then, movies were played one after another on continuous loops, with some news and a bit of advertising in between. A main feature, 'the big picture', would play first, followed by the 'B-film' or 'the little picture'. The stars in the latter were often less famous but Grandpa enjoyed them all the same.

Sometimes he'd watch several loops, remaining until dinner-time, or until he had to be dragged home. Once, when he was thirteen, his mother had to come in with the manager and a torch to fetch him out. He never grew bored with the pictures despite the fact he couldn't hear the dialogue. In its place he imagined the exchanges between characters. He used the cues from the action and invented a script in his mind to match.

The movie halls he went to—the Cosy Cinema in Coseley and the Picture House in Prince's End—played special children's broadcasts on Saturday mornings. The queues would stretch outside the doors on those days. At the Picture House, he'd fling himself over the boundary wall at the side of the property so he could get in for free. A staff member used to stand outside with a stick to keep the kids in line. When Grandpa described it, he took up the position of that man, ushering the herd with a sweep of his hand. He recalled watching *Flash Gordon* and *The Lone Ranger* in the tip-up seats at the back where the view was best.

Film played an important role in my grandparents' budding relationship, too. Before they were married, they used to meet every Wednesday at The Cinephone in Birmingham, where they'd watch foreign films with subtitles. There were many deaf people who went there for that reason. 'It was much easier for us to understand everything going on,' Grandpa explained. 'We didn't have to make it up!'

In their retirement, my grandparents stopped going to the cinema. 'Perhaps we've been spoiled by captions on telly,' Nanny suggested when I asked her about it. Cinemas today are under no obligation to play captioned films, and rarely do so. The 'Captiview' devices (often referred to as crap-ti-view), which provide access to text, are loathed by the Deaf community. Many of my Deaf friends boycott the cinema because they hate splitting their attention between the two screens. Having to do so is disruptive, and often the service is intermittent or fails entirely, leaving the viewer lost and pissed off.

Where subtitles are merely the translations of dialogue in another language, captions are the text version of speech and other sounds including laughter, descriptions of music, and sound effects. When depicting speech, the colour of the text and its position on the screen show who is speaking. There are two different types: open and closed. Open are permanent and burned into the original source. Closed are added after the program is recorded and can be turned on or off.

The history of captioning, though seldom credited as such, is linked to Deaf initiatives. The earliest attempts came about in the late 1920s by a deaf man named Emerson Romeo. With the introduction of the talkies, deaf people could no longer rely on subtitles present in silent films. Frustrated by this, Romeo, who was also an actor, began experimenting with ways of splicing text in between the talkies' footage. His crude tactics of cutting scenes with printed dialogue are now recognised as a key catalyst in developing captioning. Romeo's edited films were shared among deaf people until they caught the attention of industry figureheads.

In the United States, the first preview of captioning took place at the First National Conference on Television for the Hearing Impaired in Nashville, Tennessee in 1971. In Australia, closed captioning began on television in 1982. Until amendments to the Broadcasting Services Act were passed in 1998, there was no legislation requiring the provision of captions. During the nineties, free-to-air services were required to caption news and current affairs as well as programs screened during prime time. The shows that were captioned had a huge influence on the tastes of Deaf Australians. The soap opera *Home and Away* was one of the first non–news related programs to have captions and had a huge Deaf fan base. Nanny used to watch it every evening, not so much because she enjoyed it, but because it was accessible.

My grandparents often complained about their access to entertainment and current affairs. Frequently they'd turn something on only to find there were no captions. In those moments, the fact of their exclusion felt acute. Grandpa would throw down his remote in exasperation and Nanny would tell me then how far Australia lagged behind Britain. In 2014 it became mandatory to include captions on all content screened on free-to-air television between six a.m. and midnight, including live captioning for news. This provided some relief. But while the rule applies to major channels like SBS, ABC, Seven, Nine and Ten, it doesn't to their spinoff channels like Gem, Go and Channel 11, which often broadcast programs without them.

Captioning remains an imperfect art and is no substitute for interpreters. Live captions are the least reliable, and the quality varies depending on the provider and the technology used by broadcasters. The most common complaints relate to errors in spelling, unclear distinctions between speakers and issues with sync, sometimes with a lag of up to ten seconds between audio and caption. Grandpa used to be driven mad by malfunctioning text. He was always a pedant about language and its use, and would count the errors, huffing as they flashed across the screen.

But beyond their imprecision, English is a second language for many d/Deaf people and captions rarely give the full picture. During the bushfires of 2019–2020 and the pandemic, deaf people agitated for emergency information to be provided in Auslan. This led to the widespread use of sign language interpreting during Covid-related broadcasts. Up until then, the practice was patchy at best. Though strides have been made in this domain, there remains no legal requirement for current affairs and news programming to be interpreted, meaning that d/Deaf people whose first language is not English are routinely left out of political conversations.

Deaf and hard-of-hearing people have also been left out of pay TV, 'on-demand TV' and streaming services, which have been patchy in providing accessible content. After Netflix was sued in 2014 by the National Association of the Deaf, the company was forced to include captioning on their service. This was a landmark case for the Deaf community, but struggles persist in online spaces, which are unregulated and without safeguards to ensure the captioning of videos. Clips on YouTube and even news websites are often shared without accompanying text.

When DVDs came out, they provided my grandparents and other d/Deaf people with immediate access to films. Captioned videotapes were hard to come by, and often restricted to the most mainstream releases. In the 1970s, before these were available, my mother transcribed the entire script of *The Sound of Music* for her father, songs and all, so he needn't work to fill in the blanks. After Grandpa's death, I found the handwritten pages perfectly intact in a cupboard.

One of my grandfather's hobbies when I was a child was to record films that were broadcast with captions on television. Every week he'd check the TV guide and set a schedule for his recording. In the nineties, he was forever buying new tapes to fill, siphoning everything he could from the free-to-air service. But the explosion of DVDs stopped the habit. Unlike VHS, DVDs were subtitled across the board. Those without were the exception rather than the rule.

DVDs were trusty companions, and my grandparents had a huge collection. As a teenager, I used to wander over to borrow discs from their library. Grandpa had all the classics—*Casablanca, A Streetcar Named Desire, Some Like It Hot, Roman Holiday*, and nearly everything from Alfred Hitchcock's catalogue. Grandpa's knowledge of the greats was so devout and thorough that he used to deliver DVDs to me with accompanying bits of trivia. He had an encyclopaedic memory when it came to actors and directors, and often shared anecdotes about their lives or their repertoire of work.

I spent a lot of time as a child lying in the front room of their house as Grandpa selected viewing material for my pleasure.

Grandpa introduced me to the world of the screen. He played me stories of girls with big spirit—*Little Women*, *The Secret Garden* and *National Velvet*, and I'd request them over and over. As I grew, he trialled me on a more varied diet, granting me access to his personal favourites, many of which were comedies or silent pictures.

He loved the Carry On films and Nanny did too. Anything slapstick delighted them both: Laurel and Hardy, Benny Hill and Mr Bean. The three of us used to watch Charlie Chaplin together and would be left in stitches. Silent films are cherished in Deaf circles because of their use of text, but also their visual sensibility. When I was volunteering at a Sydney Deaf school, I observed senior students completing an analysis of *The Circus* in their English class. The laugher was uproarious. For weeks they begged the teacher to replay sections of it on YouTube. The pupils were convinced Chaplin was deaf and were incredulous when they learned he was hearing. Perhaps it was the miming, or the movements of his face, but they couldn't believe a hearing person could capture physical humour in such a 'Deaf' way.

There were only a handful of films my grandfather could give me about deafness. Along with documentaries and biopics about Helen Keller, I watched *Mr Holland's Opus* and *Children of a Lesser God*, though my grandparents never saw themselves reflected in these stories. They thought them too dramatic, too 'Hollywood-ised' to ring true.

More recently, shows like *Switched at Birth*, *Only Murders in the Building* and *Deaf U* have brought deafness into the mainstream, giving audiences access to d/Deaf characters and worlds. Ukrainian film *The Tribe* has been admired for the ways it inverts the deaf and hearing experience. The entire movie is performed in sign, and contains no voiceover or subtitles, meaning the audience is left to decipher the action with only visual cues. At the cinema, I watched it breathlessly, feeling as if I'd slipped momentarily into my grandparents' minds.

In 2022, *CODA*—a film about a deaf, sign language–using family—won best picture at the Oscars. In the audience, Hollywood stars acknowledged the milestone win by adopting the Deaf form of applause, where fingers are raised and wiggled in the air. The victory was historic, a nod in the direction of diversity. *CODA* was unique given its cast were largely deaf, and the production team consulted regularly with the Deaf community. More commonly though, representations of deafness are fraught and criticised for their reliance on tired tropes. Deaf actors are rarely hired, even for d/Deaf roles, and hearing performances of sign are often insultingly poor— misrepresentative at best, cultural appropriation at worst.

In Australia, sign language has been given a platform in children's entertainment through the efforts of Emma Watkins, the former yellow Wiggle. Emma's use of signs on stage and on screen have made a huge contribution to raising the profile of signing and deafness in the hearing world, but the impact is most profound for deaf children. Because young children cannot read captions, deaf children's access to TV shows is limited. Watching Emma means they can see their language reflected and celebrated in the world.

When I was a child, there was a Deaf presenter on ABC's *Playschool* named Sofya Gollan. While the other hosts told stories and sang songs, Sofya signed along. Seeing her was the highlight of my afternoons. Somehow her presence was a comfort—a recognition that my grandparents' ways were worthy of the screen.

•

Although I can barely remember a time when Grandpa didn't have the Sony in his hand, it wasn't until the early nineties that he first put himself behind the camera. The first home movie Grandpa took of us kids was shot in their backyard in late 1992. It shows us kids playing around their clothesline, in the middle of a game we used to play with the pegs. With the peg basket at my hip, I scatter them over the grass and then the lot of us go racing to pick them up. As with most of his films, there's no accompanying sound. Just our bodies tottering around the garden.

Before Grandpa bought his camera, my mother used to ask a family friend, Peter, to capture domestic scenes. When my sister was born, Peter came to the house. There's footage of her fast asleep in her basinet, and of me answering questions about animal sounds, sandwiched between Mum and Nanny on the couch.

When I was born, my parents hired a professional videographer to visit the hospital and document my first days. Played over close-ups of my tiny wrists and ankles is an instrumental version of 'Memories' from the musical *Cats*. As the music dies down, my parents come into view, fussing over me and taking instruction from an unflappable nurse who shows my mother how to swaddle me in a blanket. The various segments of the film are polished, edited and shaped, with smooth transitions and fades between frames.

These early tapes are markedly different from those that came after. From 1992 onwards, there's a shift both in style and content. Where Peter and the professional traced the lines of dialogue between people, flitting back and forth between interlocutors in the midst of exchange, Grandpa never followed the arc of conversations. Instead, he followed movements. Wherever there was action, so too was Grandpa's eye.

If you watch the films back, you can see it most when he captures us kids. He follows us as we race up and down the rope-stairs of our cubby houses, or as we dig in the sandpit. He lingered on James practising tricks on his skateboard, and on me singing songs to the camera. He saw our performances, but also the more mundane and quotidian things—my cousin Emily engrossed in a TV show, or Thomas cleaning his teeth at the sink.

With his camera, he documented the intimate corners of our lives, nosing his way into rooms to video everything in sight. He'd open the doors of linen presses and closets, garages and bathrooms, catching himself in the mirror as he went. He filmed all our houses and our bedrooms in forensic detail, panning over our toys and the trinkets on our bookcases, his breath whistling in the background all the while. He recorded the minutiae of places in such depth that sometimes I'm not sure if my memories of them are derived from his tapes or from my own mind.

In the past, when we were subjected to reruns of the footage, it would elicit a collective groan. We'd skip past long, dull passages of what was then familiar ground. Decades on, we watch them back with wide-eyed nostalgia for the way things were. Even my dad was pleased when I sourced a tape from the early 2000s and played it after dinner one night. Grandpa had videoed the months of renovations Dad had completed on our family home. When my father saw the footage, he reminisced about the labour it took, the materials, the setbacks, the physical toll. At the end of the viewing, he went quiet. 'Wow,' he said, 'I didn't know he'd taken all of this.'

Sometimes I think about my grandparents' life as though it were a movie, picturing it in my mind as I write. In truth, film would be a far better medium for narrating the lives of d/Deaf people. But alas, I am not a filmmaker.

When I picture it, I do so as though it's been shot on cine film, the stuff used in home movies in the mid-twentieth century. Cine film captured images alone. There was no sound in the footage. My imaginings get spliced with the real, grainy, flickering cine film I've seen of Nanny and Grandpa in England when my mum and Uncle Ray were small. I think it was taken on my great-uncle Lawson's camera.

In the Netherlands, where I lived for a time in my late teens and early twenties, they call this now-obsolete product Smalfilm, a word that, to me, makes far more sense than the English equivalent, and is apt for my grandparents' story. Their motion picture wouldn't be a blockbuster or an epic, nor a melodrama. It would be something quiet and understated, something that made you look in hidden or forgotten places, that made you see the things in the foreground and in the margins.

6.

'Music is the space between the notes.'

—*Claude Debussy*

Next to English and Auslan, music was the third language in my family. To varying degrees we all spoke it, engaged in its colloquy from the earliest age. Our home was boisterous with sound, the hallway dense with the cacophony of three competing stereos that blared daily from the bedrooms of my siblings and me.

After school, you could hear us as we practised our scales and breathing patterns, mindful of the placement of our lips and tongues around the mouthpieces of our respective instruments: Lizzie on clarinet, James on trumpet, and me, albeit briefly, on the flute. By the time I started high school, I'd switched to singing and piano lessons, and a mahogany upright took pride of place in our lounge room. Though neither of our parents were musically adept, they shared a deep respect for those who were, and their appreciation (coupled with their extensive CD collection) thrust the act of listening to the centre of our collective consciousness.

I spent much of my early childhood propped before the wall unit that held Dad's hi-fi system as he steered me through his version of the musical canon: Pink Floyd, Bowie and the Beatles. He'd sit me down on the Persian rug and lift treasured vinyl down from the shelves to show me. The unit was a monolith: a floor-to-ceiling fixture with recesses for the turntable, tuner and five-stacker CD player. Behind cupboard doors on either side were two giant speakers, and in the glass cabinets that hung like eyes in the top corners of the structure was a statue of John Lennon's head, a brass deity that peered down at us during our ceremony.

As we listened, I'd watch Dad intently for signs of revelry and wonder. Sometimes, during guitar solos or frenzied climaxes, his face seemed to break open, giving rest to his ordinarily brusque facade. In some childish act of empathic psychological mirroring, I'd adopt his facial expressions, beaming them back at him in an effort to modulate myself in his direction. I understood even then the unifying potential of music. It was a conduit: a channel to bridge even the deepest of chasms. I hung on the lilt of every refrain he showed me, filing them away as wisdom about the spectrum of human experience and, too, as fragments with which to solve the mystery he was to me.

Music offered us a window to one another, a clear streak in the glass that was, for the most part, opaque. His was a world of engine oil and grease, of hours spent working with his hands as he restored World War II–era Harley Davidsons, a hobby he later turned into a career. With my siblings, my father had more traction. They bonded over sport and athleticism, pursuits I had no skill or interest in. From the sidelines of my brother's soccer matches, or my sister's netball games, Dad would scream advice (and occasionally abuse at the ref), and I'd dive into a book, escaping into far-off worlds. Books and words were often my armour, but a hiding place too, impenetrable to my father, who was sceptical of the literary elite. But music—the type that groaned with the grit and fervour of middle-class life—offered us a meeting place, a lingua franca. My father, who rationed praise and sentiment, and who partitioned his practical and feeling selves, spoke to me freely through music. His offerings revealed a tender part of him, a part I'd often scramble to revisit. Through the songs and artists he shared, he gave voice to truths he could not speak aloud.

I'd often heard the expression that 'music is the great equaliser', universal in its ability to bring joy and consolation to those in its presence. But for all that I cherished about music—its impetus to reach both within and between selves—I could not, for many years, reconcile its place in my life with the fact of my grandparents' deafness.

As a child, I sang to them unabashedly, warbling like a magpie as I strutted through their house and pirouetted down the hallway. I was always putting on shows, and often roped the other kids into elaborate backyard productions. Before the garden beds full of brightly coloured annuals, I'd drag a plastic chair for Nanny, and subject her to renditions of my favourite Disney songs and self-made ditties that swirled through my head. Sometimes she'd misjudge the end of a performance and clap prematurely. In those instances, I'd hold up a single finger and her hands would retreat to her lap. As I reached the crescendo and trilled the final note, I'd meet her gaze and nod. With that signal, my grandmother would erupt into generous rounds of applause, and I'd bow and curtsey with her fanfare.

Grandpa would often venture outside to film our performances. He'd hover above us, capturing footage as we tooted our recorders or howled into plastic echo microphones, the kind that sound like thunder when you shake them. Flagging him down with a wave of my arm, I'd deliver songs down the barrel of the camera, draping myself round the pole of the Hills hoist for dramatic effect. Grandpa filmed James on the trumpet and Ben as the Master of Ceremonies. He filmed our annual 'Christmas Day Concerts' (directed by me), where I'd coax the other kids into nativity-themed costumes as we sang carols and acted out the story of Jesus's birth. Most of the videos have no sound. Having no need for the audio himself, he often forgot to record with the volume turned up, meaning that reels of our past are preserved much as he saw it, as a silent motion picture.

At family barbecues, we used to have whole family dance parties before bed. Dad or Ray would crank the stereo and us kids would jump around until we dropped. Those ad-hoc discos were among my favourite pastimes as a child, and I used to beg the grownups to spin and twirl me round. I have no memory of Nanny and Grandpa joining in. But they would have been there, no doubt watching the fun.

It wasn't until my adolescence that I began withdrawing my musicality from my grandparents' view. It happened in stages, in unspoken, sometimes unconscious retreats from their gaze. At thirteen, I was still in the habit of rehearsing in their house, practising vocal exercises into the quiet. At Nanny and Grandpa's, I could sing as loud and hard as I wanted without fear of my brother yelling down the hall at me to shut up. Against the walls of their home, I threw my voice around, played with it, made it dance into higher registers and sink into chesty growls. I let the melodies waft and tumble, soar, scream and even cry. But the further I delved into that training, the more it began to feel illicit, perhaps even harmful.

For a time, I had a plastic Casio keyboard stored atop the chest of drawers in their spare bedroom, where I spent hours labouring over consonant arrangements of chords and lyrics. As I played, Nanny would pop her head round the door, bringing cups of pineapple juice to sustain me. My singing teacher had told me it was good for vocal health, so Nanny began buying it in bulk. Resting the juice on the dresser, Nanny would sit on the bed and watch as I ran my fingers up and down the keys. I'd feel her eyes upon me, and my stomach would lurch. Over the course of that year, my visits to the spare room petered out. Eventually, Nanny asked if she might move the keyboard to a less conspicuous place. I disconnected the cords and shoved it under the bed, where it remained gathering dust for several years afterwards.

I didn't have words for the things I felt then, only a leaden guilt. I began to develop partitions of my own: there were spaces for music, and spaces for Nanny and Grandpa. At school and in my living room I carried on singing and writing songs on the piano. I spent my lunchtimes in the music department jamming with the junior rock band and the head teacher, who often stayed back to play with the keener students. I became a regular performer at school presentation nights and open days, singing at the local club and rotary events. But with my grandparents, I kept my passion hushed and cloaked from view, shoving it downwards like it was a dark and unutterable secret. I didn't tell them about my entrance into talent competitions, nor did I tell them when I got a lead role in the school musical. I worried (perhaps ironically) that exposure to music would make them feel left out; that my love of it was somehow disloyal. Through omission, I thought I could buffer the sharp edges of my behaviour. I erected a bulwark to preserve their feelings, and to guard against any hurt I might inflict.

In my grandmother I'd discerned a kind of longing, a desire for access to a culture that so often evaded her grasp. I saw its traces in the times she sat with me, fingering the pieces of sheet music strewn around the room, which contained the strange and inde-cipherable symbols I was learning to read. She'd point at the little squiggles on the pages, the latticed lines of the staff or the coil of the treble clef, and ask me what they mean. Sometimes I could explain, and Nanny would nod, but other times I watched her face go blank and felt myself at an impasse.

In those teen years, I saw only limits in the ways my grand-mother grappled and mused over my talent. She reasoned once that music must be in my blood, handed down to me from her side of the family. Nanny's Auntie Gladys was an opera singer and pianist who played for her local church. Everyone said she should have been famous. When Nanny spoke of our likeness, I stiffened. With a pang, perhaps of grief, I'd fumble to articulate the differ-ence between opera and my own pop-folk style. I'd return home, heavy and thrown, believing that Nanny's deafness precluded her from me, and from the particulars of my world. Back then, music and love were so deeply intertwined, I feared that a lack of literacy in one might mar or even eliminate the other.

There was something of misplaced guilt and grief in my mother, too. Whenever she drove with her parents in tow, she habitually turned off the car radio. It was a gesture of courtesy, lest she offend by flaunting the spoils of a life with sound. I know that a family friend of ours, Chris, who is hearing and grew up with deaf parents and a deaf sister, used to flee the house to listen to music. It felt wrong to be in his bedroom enjoying it while his family was down-stairs. With his boombox on his shoulder, he'd cycle to the canal and blast the Top 40 charts on his own, returning to his relatives at the end of his sonic excursion. When my mother heard Chris's story, she sighed in recognition. 'Growing up, I think I always felt guilty,' she said. When I asked her what she felt guilty of, she gulped and replied, 'Of being able to hear.'

The world, and the music I'd come to know with my ears, was unimaginable to me any other way. And when I think now of the lines I drew between my grandparents and me, and the ways I policed our difference, I find myself reflecting on the only public performance I ever allowed them to attend.

I was seventeen and seated on a makeshift stage behind a piano. A PA system hummed in the background as I adjusted my microphone, causing it to feed back and send a high-pitched squeal through the speakers. The whole room cringed in unison, our shoulders scrunched in defence of our ears. All except Nanny and Grandpa. I was the final performer of the night, and when I descended the stage, I was swarmed with well-wishers. Through a break in the crowd, I saw Nanny hovering on the sidelines, waiting for contact. We smiled at one another and her face lit up, knowing she had my attention. She didn't move or try to push past the people clustered around me, but quickly mouthed, 'I love you.' I held her gaze for a moment before catching sight of Grandpa. His video camera hung at his side, and he was laughing at the sight of a red-headed toddler thrashing the strings of his older brother's guitar.

In that moment, their deafness seemed the most heinous injustice. I wanted them to hear. I wanted them to hear so much that I could scarcely look at them for the entire journey home.

Years later my grandmother described to me how I looked on the stage that night. We sat across from one another on the back deck of our home—cups of tea in hand—and she remembered how my long, straight hair was swept over to one side, spilling over my left eye whenever I leaned towards the piano. In a mixture of sign and spoken English she told me how the speakers pumped vibrations straight through her chest and limbs. By puffing out her cheeks she emulated the resonance of the bass, and with her hands she showed me how it travelled through the floor and up into her feet. She said, with unwavering certitude, she could tell I had a wonderful voice. She could see it in the way my face moved under the spotlight.

'You helped me to imagine,' she said, taking my hand in hers.

'Imagine what?' I asked.

'Music. I may be wrong, but in my head I can sense something like ups and downs, you know?' Nanny used gestures to animate it for me, rolling her hand across the air as through simulating the motion of a wave. 'It isn't flat,' she said. 'I can tell that it's beautiful. It makes me think of beautiful things.'

7.

When I first suggested writing about my grandparents' lives, my grandfather's brow furrowed. 'Who'd be bothered about people like us?' he said and cast his eyes to the ground. Nanny was elated, flattered. 'Ooh, we'll be famous,' she joked, and burst into a repertoire of poses, propping her chin on her hands as though a photographer stood waiting to take her portrait.

In the years that followed, my grandmother revelled in her role as orator. Between our lunches and shopping dates, our time together was thick with story. Without prompting or direction, Nanny provided her every memory, bouncing from idea to idea, occasionally going down rabbit holes I'd need to draw her out of.

My interest in her past provided her a platform, and much to the irritation of my family members, Nanny went on and on, repeating tales that had long become common knowledge. I lapped it up, savouring the different rhetorical flourishes that came in the re-tellings. I loved observing the liberties she took with her performances, the ways she leaned into the delivery, pausing for emphasis, conjuring pictures with her hands. Her narration was so lyrical, I often felt I was being led through paintings or lucid dreams.

But sometimes it was as though she took all the air in the room. She'd speak over the top of Grandpa, or answer questions for him. She was such a natural leading lady, foisting herself into and then basking in the spotlight, that I found myself having to manage her; I'd reminded her about taking turns, and that I was there to speak with them both.

At first, my grandfather remained in the background. I wasn't sure how he felt about me digging into his past. When I wrote a short piece about Nanny and Grandpa for a memoir class I took at university, I brought it to him for fact-checking. His only comments related to punctuation. But the following day, when I arrived at breakfast, I learned he'd circulated the essay to his Deaf friends, one who later had it published in a Deaf magazine in the United States. In preparation for my arrival, Grandpa had collected pictures and newspaper articles, and placed them in a manila folder for me. 'You might be needing some of these,' he said, and smiled.

When given the floor, Grandpa was the real storyteller. His semantic memory was always exceptional and meant he could recite verses of poetry and literature off the top of his head. He retained odd facts and dates, storing them with careful precision in the warehouse of his mind.

As a child, I often sat with Grandpa while he told me tales of his childhood. Long before I started asking about it, he used to recount the family holidays he took to Blackpool: the rock candy and the arcades; the air raids during years of the war; the military insignia he knew to look for on the planes. More than anything, though, he liked to tell of the mischief Mum and Uncle Ray got up to when they were small, how my mother once tied my uncle to a chair and left him for hours screaming for help. Ray called out to no avail, of course. Nanny and Grandpa couldn't hear his cries. He stayed there until dinner when Nanny came searching upstairs.

Though we traded almost exclusively in stories, there was a wordlessness to my exchanges with Grandpa. Usually, he read his paper from his armchair perch. But sometimes, especially if I was sad, we'd sit together on the lounge, our noses in our respective books. Ever the autodidact, Grandpa was always reading. He'd frequently consult his encyclopaedias and reference books whenever he found himself wondering about one thing or another. It was a habit he developed in childhood, having found himself excluded, often unintentionally, from family conversations. Books provided sanctuary and the stimulation he so craved.

At our family dinners, especially the boisterous variety, Grandpa would drift around the room idly picking up ornaments and inspecting them. If there were birthday or Christmas cards on the mantel, he'd devour them all.

He used to hang around the kitchen, scouring the cluster of condiments that accompanied the spread at the table. For years, he'd been in the habit of reading the fine print on the back of foodstuffs. With his glasses pinned to the bridge of his nose he'd hold up jars of jam, or bottles of sauce, and deduce what he could from the label. Over the years, he had familiarised himself with enough barcodes to ascertain the item's country of origin from the UPC code alone. I once asked him what he was doing, and he explained via demonstration. 'Look at the first number,' he directed, pointing to a cluster of digits beneath the black lines. A nine at the front meant it was made in Australia, while a four meant it was made in England.

Because I'd happened to ask, Grandpa regularly included me in his barcode antics. On the surface it was an odd pastime, but as years went by, I began to see it as an adaptive strategy—a remedy for boredom and isolation.

When I was a teenager, Grandpa once read my diary after I left it unattended on their dining table. I'd gone to the bathroom, only to return and find him leafing through it. I flew into a rage, snatching it from him and storming home. Later, when Nanny coaxed me back there, Grandpa must have apologised but all I remember is his face. It was ashen; a look of bewilderment cast a shadow over his features. Back then, I saw my grandfather's behaviour as a violation. Years on, I see this as a moment of cultural clash. Here was a man who read everything in his path, why not an unidentified notebook that was left in his house?

·

The diary incident was jarring, especially because my grandfather was otherwise considered, deliberate in all he did. Grandpa paid attention to my preferences, perhaps because they often overlapped with his. Knowing I loved toffees as much as he did, Grandpa used to save them up and sneak them my way when Nanny wasn't looking. We'd laugh and shove them into our mouths, slipping the wrappers down the side of the lounge until we had a clear path to the bin. Much later, when he'd been diagnosed with type 2 diabetes, he gave me the remains of his stash—the now-forbidden spoils of several birthday and Christmas gifts.

My grandmother's love was viscous, fervent and outward-facing. But my grandfather's tenderness was found in small acts of generosity. When Grandpa first got a computer, he'd print Wikipedia pages for us all. If we spoke about something in the days prior, you could guarantee a relevant printout would soon follow. It was always that way with him. He committed the details of previous conversations to memory and found ways to build on whatever you offered him.

When I was small, my grandfather sometimes frightened me, as did other men. My father always had a quick temper, and my pop and uncles (besides Ray) were aloof, and rarely paid me much attention. Grandpa was not like the others, but his voice, when it was raised, alarmed me. It was rare that he yelled intentionally, but his volume control was minimal at best, and sometimes I mistook it for rage.

Whenever I stayed the night at Nanny and Grandpa's, I'd watch my morning cartoons beside their gas fire, which smelled perennially of dust and chemicals. In the winter, I would splay myself across the carpet, lying as close as I could to the red panels of heat. Grandpa would look up and see me virtually on top of the thing, and his voice would come booming in my direction. 'Get away from that fire!' he'd bark at a thousand decibels. 'You'll catch alight!' At this, I would recoil as though I'd been struck. Grandpa would eye me quizzically, puzzled by my reaction.

Seeing me hunched in the corner, he'd soften his face and posture, and liken me to a 'pussycat', reciting the words to a nursery rhyme:

'Pussycat, pussycat where have you been?

I've been to London to visit the Queen

Pussycat, pussycat, what did you there?

I frightened a little mouse under the chair.'

Gently, slowly, he waited for my fear to lift. When he thought me ready, he extended his hand, bringing me back to safety.

As I grew, the heater remained a sticking point between us. Soon, I became precocious enough to answer back when he told me to move. Where once I'd have shifted on command, I eventually learned to fold my arms and stick my nose in the air: an act of temerity that made him roll his eyes and shake his head. 'You're just like your mother,' he'd say, and I was never quite sure if he referred to our reptilian love of heat, or of our defiance in the face of men telling us what to do.

In the years I spent researching deafness, Grandpa became my co-pilot. He sourced books, DVDs and many a Wikipedia page. For a time, a few months perhaps, I left the topic of the book unbroached, leaving space for him to think it over. One day, as we sat on the back deck drinking tea, Grandpa asked me when my 'masterpiece' would be finished. I laughed and told him I hadn't started.

I asked him if I should. And whether he'd rather write something himself. Grandpa shook his head.

'You do it,' he said. 'I'd like that very much.'

Grandpa was mentally agile until the last. Reading eventually fatigued him, but he continued to watch quiz shows religiously. It seemed cruel that a mind so sharp was locked in a body so worn out. For years, we agonised over Grandpa's ailing health, reminding him to take his puffers and use his emergency personal alarm when he needed help. His list of medications was unwieldy, and his frequent stints in hospital meant there were many close calls and false alarms. On several occasions I found myself enfeebled by a kind of anticipatory grief.

I had time to imagine the world without my grandfather in it. I'd been documenting my grandparents' stories for some years before he died, and my PhD thesis in Deaf and Disability Studies was inspired by them.

As Grandpa grew sicker, the urge to preserve and the guilt for intruding were constantly jostling for space within me. I could never quite tell what state I would find him in—which version of my grandfather I'd receive on any given day. There were times it seemed he was bursting out of his skin. Itching to tell me things. For Nanny, too, there was urgency. It was as if she'd waited a lifetime for an audience. Grandpa's face would light up when I appeared at the door of The Cottage. 'Question time again?' he'd ask, with a grin, and I'd feel as though I were expanding. Other days he tired quickly, growing flustered when he couldn't keep up. 'No questions today, please,' he'd say in a soft, defeated voice. 'It's too much.' On particularly black days, he'd sleep while I spoke to Nanny.

Over the many years of my grandfather's decline, long before the heart attack and the weeks in palliative care, it seemed as if time was evaporating: that any moment I could lose him.

When he was gone, it felt nothing like I'd imagined. There was some relief, but mostly, I was stunned, frozen. I cycled erratically through grief. The stages people talked about—denial, anger, bargaining, depression and acceptance—seemed to be all out of order for me. The pain of it was something animal.

For several months I existed under its cloud, surfacing in brief moments. I visited the family home more often, making sure to check on Mum and Nanny. In company I could dedicate myself to other causes, but alone, my grief was trammelling. Some days I was content to wear it on my sleeve and other days it felt indulgent. Much like my mother, I found myself asking if I could have done more for him. I worried that a granddaughter's grief should be milder, more contained.

It has been said that guilt and anger are different sides of the same coin: opposing but interrelated states. I found myself thrashing between the two, trying to make good on ways I might have failed him, and possessed with a childlike fury at being left behind. The rage was despairing and other times hot and barbed. Eventually it pointed in the direction of something bigger, less tangible behind the injustices of my grandfather's life.

Soon enough, I found myself leafing through books about bereavement. Among them was the work of psychologist David Kessler. Though Kessler had researched and written extensively about grief, it wasn't until he suddenly lost his twenty-one-year-old son that he realised that the five stages of grief were missing a final step: meaning.

'Meaning,' he suggests, 'is the sixth stage of grief, where the healing often resides.' Kessler elaborates, 'Ultimately, meaning comes through finding a way to sustain your love for the person after their death while you're moving forward with your life.' I was struck by the idea of that final phase. There was something too in his insistence that grief must be witnessed, must be observed through social rituals, that turned remembering into a radical act.

When Grandpa died, Uncle Ray inherited his watch and the family Bible. My mum was given a crimson and gold hardcover copy of *David Copperfield* that belonged to my great-great-grandmother. Her name, Lizzie Bird, is written on the inner sleeve. Mum was also given an antique dinner gong that my great-great-grandfather bought on his travels with the marines. It sits on a side table in our lounge room and my nieces love to strike it and listen as it rings out, just as I did when it lived at Nanny and Grandpa's.

Nothing material was handed down to us kids. We wanted everything else to remain with Nanny. But I became the keeper of Grandpa's papers. The manila folder he gave me became a kind of archive. In the years leading up to his death, it ballooned so large that I needed to transfer the various photos, jottings and sheets of correspondence into a drawer in my sideboard.

One night, about three months after he died, I spread its contents over the floor of my apartment. From my perch on the couch, they looked like pieces of a patchwork quilt my grandmother might have made. I surveyed the loose ends of his life: the reams of yellowed paper and the hurried scrawl of Grandpa's handwriting. I wondered how I might stitch them all together, before stuffing them back into the drawer. They remained there, untouched for another six months. I wasn't sure how to begin, but my grandfather's stories were alive in my mind, and they needed a place to rest.

8.

My grandfather lost his hearing in the Royal Hospital, Wolverhampton, during the spring of 1940. He was eight. A month beforehand, he'd been playing war games with his cousins in the streets. At the end of the cul-de-sac where he lived, there was an old, dilapidated building the kids used as a makeshift battlefield. They darted around the rubble throwing rocks at one another, pretending they were shells being hurled across the trenches. A stone hit my grandfather in his left eye, and he was taken to the Royal for treatment. His mother was beside herself and feared he'd end up blind. 'You'll be the death of me!' she told him then, cupping his cheeks in her hands. His sight was unaffected, and Grandpa went home with a warning. A few weeks later, he returned to hospital, this time deathly ill with meningitis.

On the day Grandpa fell sick, he and his mother were visiting his grandma, and the neighbour whom he called Auntie Law had popped over for tea. He lay on his grandmother's couch and shivered uncontrollably, listening to the concerned whispers of the three women as they hovered above him, contemplating what to do. He was taken home to bed, his mother checking on him. The next morning, he refused his boiled egg and toast, and soon became unresponsive. An ambulance was called, and he was whisked away on a stretcher. In those days there was no National Health Service and his parents had to pay half a crown for the ambulance.

For several days he drifted in and out of consciousness, wracked with fever and muscle pain. He had no concept of how long he stayed in the ward, only that it took him a year to learn to walk again, and that somewhere in the walls of that place, he went deaf.

Grandpa never recounted this as trauma. Whenever he spoke of it, his tone was unvarnished. His memories were those of a child and were steeped in the forbearance and naivety of that child-self. I waited for him to tell me of the moment the silence descended upon him, to give me a glimpse of his terror or shock. But for him, there was no such moment.

Parts of the memories were foggy and insensible, appearing to him in brief snatches. There were chunks of time too that remained blank in his mind—months unaccounted for, information never divulged. But he remembered the doctors checking his ears, and the nurses at night flitting through the corridors like ghosts in their white caps and aprons. There was one night he fell from his hospital bed, not realising he could no longer walk. I imagined his boyish frame in a crumpled heap on the linoleum floor, and the confusion that must have followed.

He spoke too of the boredom, the drear of passing time with nothing to do. Early in his stay, the nurses confiscated his comics— although he wasn't sure why—and the days stretched out before him without end. In the ward he shared with ten to fifteen men, he spent much time alone and without interaction. His bed was closest to the window and had a view of the Wolverhampton Corporation Bus Depot over the road. He spent hours watching the dusty green double-deckers rolling in and out of the garage, the motion of the wheels breaking the stillness and monotony of the days. He grew privy to their comings and goings, content to see their noses sneak out from the kerb and teeter onto the road. There was comfort in seeing them return at nightfall, lumbering their way into the yard to rest. Without sound, he learned to observe, and after that was fascinated with automation and things that move.

As part of his treatment, Grandpa had to have three injections in his bottom. On the third injection he protested, and the nurse, upon seeing his distress, thought to write him a note. 'This is the last one,' she scrawled on a piece of scrap paper, and Grandpa let her proceed. It was much later that he realised why she'd written it down at all. 'It's strange,' he told me. 'I never realised I'd gone deaf.' I asked if anyone had explained it to him at the time. What about the doctors? His parents? He told me no, but perhaps they had tried and failed. After all, he couldn't hear what they were saying.

On the day he was discharged, he travelled home in a car. During the journey, he turned to his mother and said, 'This car must be very good. It's ever so quiet.' He remembered telling one of the nurses about noises he heard in his head, haunting refrains of music that came and went during the day. 'I told the nurse, "I can hear someone playing the piano under my pillow." She said, "Well, carry on listening." She must have known, but she didn't tell me.'

These auditory hallucinations, or 'phantasmal noises', persisted in the months of his recovery. They are thought to be common, especially in people who become deaf post-lingually. Phantom auditory events can even be induced temporarily in hearing people after experiencing severe auditory deprivation, like stepping inside an anechoic chamber, for example. The 'noises' have no external source but are a form of tinnitus.

Once, when he was home, he thought he heard his mother scream from the kitchen. So convinced by the faithfulness of that imagined sound, my grandfather hauled himself from bed. Still unable to walk, he dragged his limp body down the hall to reach her, using his elbows to crawl along the floor. But when he arrived, she was fine. Another time, he thought his dad was crying out from behind the bathroom door. Though his mother tried, Grandpa could not be calmed until the door was opened, revealing his father to be perfectly well.

It wasn't until my grandfather's first day of school since the illness that he fully comprehended the fact of his deafness. No longer able to attend the local hearing school, he was sent to the Royal School for Deaf Children in Edgbaston, Birmingham, where he boarded during the week. Many schools for deaf children at that time were boarding schools, which meant that children forged unique and important bonds with one another but spent much time away from their families. Grandpa's place at school was funded by the government, as was common in the UK at the time. His working-class parents were spared financial burden but felt the emotional cost of letting him go. Though Grandpa could have been sent across the country to schools with more competitive reputations, his parents chose Edgbaston because it was close: about half an hour from their house in Coseley. It was near enough to their home that they could visit or bring him back on weekends.

Grandpa told me about his shock upon seeing sign language for the first time, how he stood encircled by other pupils and tried and failed to communicate. This part of the story he told entirely in sign, with no English accompaniment. Pointing to himself he made the sign for 'speak': both hands raised to the mouth with two fingers pressed twice against the thumb, moving out from the lips as though pulling a rope in the direction of sound. Then, he showed me the other boys signing to him. Pivoting his shoulders to mark a perspective shift, he brought me back to his point of view, using the sign for 'look' paired with a strained facial expression. He propped an elbow atop his left hand, and with a clenched fist, showed how he nodded his head, feigning his way through conversations.

Eventually Grandpa picked up the language, being immersed in the new environment, but it must have taken months for him to fully adjust. On the first night he boarded, Grandpa cried himself to sleep beneath the covers of his dormitory bed.

By the time Grandpa had fully integrated into the school and the language, he had learned the ways of his peers. After bedtime in the dorms, one of the boys would produce a smuggled torch and they'd play cards under the cover of night. As they signed to one another, chatting and playing, one the boys would stand guard at the door, keeping an eye out for any incoming foot traffic.

For my grandma, who went deaf at six months old after a bout of pneumonia, there was no such adaptation to contend with. She has no memories of sound. Grandpa became deaf, whereas Nanny, as far as her memory stretches, always was. Perhaps because I know what it is to hear, I was always fascinated by the way Grandpa went deaf. As a child, I made him recount the events again and again. I was entranced by the idea of a boarding school, but somehow, not being able to make the distinction, imagined him living in an orphanage. For years, I could not watch the film *Oliver*, which happened to be one of Grandpa's favourites, without getting upset. But his reflections on his time at the Royal also felt like an origin story. It was a tale that explained, in part, how my grandfather came to be.

•

In Grandpa's final months, I found myself reflecting on the extended stays in hospital that bookended his life. His first and last steps as a deaf man played out against a medical backdrop. Though many people's lives begin and end in hospital, the symmetry of the two experiences weighed heavily. After several weeks of being bedridden, Grandpa lost the necessary muscles to walk even a few paces. In the respiratory ward where many of his last days were spent, Grandpa's bed was farthest from the window, and the screens between patients meant he couldn't see out even if he craned his neck.

Often, he requested reports from the outside world. He would sit up and ask about the weather: 'Is it raining? Sunny? Windy?' I would offer to take him out. There were always other men coming and going with oxygen tanks fixed to their chairs. But Grandpa shrugged and said it was too much trouble. Instead, we watched quiz shows on the pay TV above the bed.

My grandfather and the rest of my family had grown used to the stark whiteness of hospital walls. We were accustomed to certain contraptions and procedures—nebulisers, puffers, electro-cardiograms, chest x-rays. During that final stay I was often impressed by the way that Grandpa would wake, disturbed by a nurse's poking and prodding, and immediately surrender an arm in anticipation of the blood test or blood-pressure check to come. But even with seventy-odd years between the meningitis and his death, deafness seemed no more familiar to the medical staff taking care of him.

The emergency doctor assigned to Grandpa after his heart attack was reluctant to tell him he was dying. Though Grandpa was alert and asking us questions, the doctor saw no need to inform his patient. It was only at our insistence that Grandpa was told at all. He was the last to know. My grandfather died much in the way he had lived: with patience for a world that misunderstood and often denied his autonomy.

.

I have tried to separate my grandfather's story from tropes of grief and trauma, the kind of social scripts my grandparents would roll their eyes at. In doing so, I've focused on the richness of Nanny and Grandpa's lives—on presence, rather than absence. But though I have tried, I cannot uncouple them entirely. At least not when I think of Grandpa's mother, Lily.

For many parents of deaf children, grief is an uncomfortable part of the equation. The moment they learn of their child's deafness is often the moment they relinquish their dreams and imaginings for that child's future. For parents in the twenty-first century, this often takes place at the point of newborn hearing screening, where they watch their child 'fail' the first test they've ever taken.

Until her death, Lily searched in vain for a cause for her son's deafness. She wanted rhyme or reason—an explanation for the meningitis that almost killed her child. Perhaps she wanted something or someone to blame. For many years she maintained that the rock must have carried bacteria to his brain, but her theory was never substantiated. I have spoken with several doctors about the likelihood of a child contracting meningitis from such an injury. Some have said it is plausible but unlikely. We can never know.

I cannot erase the fury from my mother's experience, either. At the end of his life, she watched on and protested as doctors failed to communicate with her father. On days we couldn't get to the hospital, Grandpa went without meals. He could not feed himself and the staff did not understand his requests for help. On one occasion, Mum arrived to find Grandpa slumped forward in a chair, his gown gaping at the chest. He was freezing and exhausted. For a full day he had been left without a buzzer for the nurse. Without it, and in the absence of making a scene, he was practically rendered mute.

When she was little, Mum hated her father's smoking habit and took to ripping up his cigarettes. On one occasion she destroyed an entire packet, and upon seeing Grandpa's rage, blamed her younger brother. She used to tell this story and we'd laugh at her gall. But in later years, especially when Grandpa's respiration rate reached over forty breaths a minute, the tale took on a different tone.

My grandfather would probably tell you that the medical team and palliative care staff did their best. He'd also reason that because of his age, they probably just assumed he was hard of hearing, despite the fact that his chart said otherwise. Maybe he'd say that both of these stays were but blips in a rich and varied life. Yet since he died, I've found myself fixating on the structures that governed so much of his life. My grandfather's needs, his very humanity, never felt more at risk than in medical spaces. The hospital cast a shadow long enough to engulf him and all he stood for. Grandpa excused the nurses who forgot him, the doctors who patronised him or couldn't be bothered trying to communicate, but I could not. When I think of him, ignored and invisible in the ward, I want to pluck him from the scene and take him someplace safe—a place where his voice might be heard.

9.

'Music, after all, is not notes and tones, but
the deceptively difficult act of listening.'

—Christopher DeLaurenti

Six months after my grandfather died, I found myself listening to old
audio files of his voice. I'd recorded them on my phone in the years
prior, whenever Grandpa decided to tell me stories about the past.
When I first revisited the recordings on my phone, I hesitated.
My finger hovered over the play button. As I heard him coming
through the speaker, my stomach lurched. I had imagined that I
would want to press my ear to the sound, play him back, again and
again. But I couldn't. It was too loud. Too acute.

If Grandpa were an instrument, he would be a trombone. His
voice boomed and reverberated in any setting, the sudden vocal
outbursts abrupt and horn-like. A few times, while in the car with
him, I was so startled by his bellowing of directions, I nearly crashed
into oncoming traffic. Post-lingually deaf, his voice had a broader
range of pitch than my grandma's. Hearing people often understood

him with ease and were shocked to hear his British Black Country accent, still unmistakable after so many years.

Nanny's voice is softer, more monotone. Though she has neither the range nor the dynamics Grandpa possessed, her voice, to me, has the richness of a cello.

When Nanny speaks, it's as though she hums. The sound resonates in her throat and nose, propelled by air in the chest rather than the belly. There is a legato quality to her phrasing, a velvety warmth to her timbre. There's a certain roundness to its sound, one you imagine being produced by a bow, not by the plucking of fingers. To other people, Nanny's speech sounds muffled, slurred and inchoate, as though listening to a voice underground or in another room. A friend once remarked it was like listening to a piano with the dampener pedal engaged.

My grandparents were fascinated by voices and often asked me to assess how well their deaf friends spoke. It used to irk me, being forced to rank and categorise people in this way, but Nanny would insist. She wanted to know how they compared.

My grandmother has always been curious and shy about her own voice. She asks me on occasion what she sounds like, reminding me that though Grandpa was the better speaker, she is the better lipreader.

When Grandpa was alive, they operated as a tag team. Nanny would defer to Grandpa on occasions where her speech was misunderstood, and Grandpa looked to Nanny for translations of a hearing person's response. This symbiosis became more pronounced after a car accident sent my grandfather blind in his right eye in 2007. The impact of the crash detached his retina, and despite seven operations, he remained without sight in that eye for the last decade of his life. Wherever they went—the grocery store, the doctor's surgery, the chemist—they were always together, filling in the blanks for one another as needed. For the times their method failed, Nanny kept a pen and a notepad in her handbag.

Like most children, I learned to speak by listening to and mimicking the sounds that my parents made. My first words were 'mama', 'dada', and 'baba'. Nanny learned to speak with chalk-dust and mirrors. Her first word was 'pig'. She was three years old.

At her school in Birmingham, my grandma was a star pupil. She attended the Moseley Road School for the Deaf, a day school that came highly recommended by the specialist who diagnosed her deafness. Her education was rooted firmly in the tradition of oralism, a medico-pedagogy which forbids the use of sign language so that pupils rely exclusively on speaking, reading lips and auditory training. If you were caught signing on school premises, you had to report to the headmistress. At the age of two and a half, Nanny began intensive speech and lipreading classes.

When I asked my grandmother about her memories of these years, she paused and lay her palms in her lap. 'We had to blend into the big hearing world,' she said, 'so we were taught to speak.' Contemplating how best to explain, she leaned towards me and took my hand. She positioned it on my nose.

'Say "N",' she instructed, performing the motion alongside me. I made the sound and it rang in my nasal cavities.

'I learned about sounds through feeling, see?' She shuffled closer and relocated my hand to my throat.

'Say "Mmm".'

I brought my lips together to make the sound and felt the vibrations ripple through my neck against my fingers.

At the front of my grandmother's classroom was a large mirror that sat next to the blackboard. Her English language teacher,

Miss Rhodes, wrote letters on the slate and Nanny had to repro-
duce the associated sound, monitoring her reflection as she went.
In these one-on-one lessons, Nanny remembers chalk powder being
sprinkled onto the back of her hands. This technique taught her
the difference between a 'b' and a 'p' sound.

'Let me show you,' she said. 'We had to have our hands like this.'

Nanny's hand was flat—fingers outstretched, palm faced down.
She brought it to her mouth, then splayed her thumb and forefinger
across her chin, her bottom lip nestled into the dorsal surface of her
hand. Pointing to a patch of skin just before the wrist, she showed
me where the chalk was placed. The white powder, when a 'p' sound
was produced, would scatter into the air. For a 'b', it wouldn't move.
'That's how you knew you were doing it right,' she told me.

Nanny remembers the first time her parents heard her speak.
She was three. The school organised a presentation day, and parents
were invited to come and witness their children's progress. 'We
had to go on stage,' Nanny told me. Each student was assigned a
placard. Printed on its front was a word in capital letters.

'I walked down the stage and held up my sign. My word was
"pig". I said it out loud. I saw my mum and dad in the audience.
Mum was crying.'

My grandmother's speech and elocution lessons weren't unusual
for their time. Many deaf pupils sat through countless hours of this
kind of educational therapy. Though the methods differed from school
to school—I've read about tissues and candle flames being used as
visual aids in some places to teach children about vocal control and the
movement of sound—the underlying principles were the same. Deaf
children needed to assimilate, and that meant they needed to speak.

Before oralism, the dominant mode of instructing deaf children
was manualism, where sign language was used in the classroom

setting. In France and the United States, signing was embraced in the eighteenth century by both teachers and students. But in 1880, following the Milan Conference on the Education of Deaf Children, educators passed resolutions that prohibited the use of sign languages in schools.

In much of the world, sign language was then suppressed until the late twentieth century. In fact, until the 1960s, sign languages were deemed to be mere supplements to spoken languages. Sign was understood as a bunch of primitive gestures—as rudimentary ideographic systems rather than a cluster of natural languages in their own right.

Deaf people refer to this period as 'the dark ages' and Deaf and Disability Studies scholars discuss the systemic violence of 'phonocentrism', our near-maniacal cultural obsession with speech, locating it as part of the project of restoring the deaf to humanity. Oralism legitimised the suppression of sign languages, and its legacy is felt to the present day. Even now, auditory–verbal programs remain near-ubiquitous for deaf children, with signing often an afterthought or seen as a last resort.

Many older deaf people remember their early school years as some of the most difficult and traumatic of their lives. For some, oralism resulted in many gruelling hours of training with limited results. In schools like my grandmother's, deaf children were beaten, called 'apes', had their hands bound behind their backs for daring to use their native language. Nanny was fortunate. Her teachers, especially Miss Rhodes, were kind and never threatened physical harm.

My grandmother reflects at times on her love for her old teacher: 'We understood one another, no trouble.' I've heard her express similar sentiments following positive interactions with other hearing people. The relief of successful communication is so great at times that she'll mull over it for days: her judgements of the other person hinging less on their actual traits, and more on their ability to decipher her speech.

I often found myself assuring my grandparents of my love for their voices. I was always fond of their vocal quirks—the way that Nanny says 'jar-a-can-dah' instead of jacaranda, or when Grandpa used to say 'wait a bit', the 't' sound would ring out at the end of the sentence as though it had been snagged on his tongue and teeth.

I loved too when they'd occasionally phrase something in the structure and syntax of sign language. 'Mum birthday what?' Nanny would ask, looking for gift ideas, and somehow, the sound of it was a comfort.

For many deaf people, the question of voice is not straightforward or uniform. There's a whole host of different preferences when it comes to communication styles, and the act of 'speaking', or choosing not to, is inherently political. I have friends who refuse to converse in the hearing way and use sign language exclusively. I've never heard them vocalise beyond laughter or the occasional outcry when drunk. Some are simply not comfortable making sounds. Others chop and change depending on their company.

Writing in the mid-twentieth century, French philosopher Jacques Derrida critiqued our social understanding of voice. He argued it had come to be synonymous with Western ideas of truth, being and presence. In other words, speaking was akin to being. In his view, this had subordinated the written word to speech. He didn't mention sign language.

From the 1960s, when William Stokoe published his mono-graph, 'Sign Language Structure', speech and language could no longer be collapsed into one. Stokoe's findings confirmed sign languages to be complex, complete languages. This disturbed previous orthodoxies that considered sign to be mere mime, and sparked an intellectual revolution. We now know that infants develop manual or signed language just as easily as a spoken language, and that the same part of the brain used for speech processing is used to process sign. Hearing babies now dabble in baby sign while their deaf peers are actively discouraged from doing the same. And still we cannot let go of the primacy of the voice as located in the mouth, lips, tongue and throat.

My old singing teacher used to say that the voice is a muscle. If you don't use it, you lose it. When you learn to sing, as I did as a child, you become conscious of how your mouth functions as a chamber, paying particular attention to the various ways that sound can be produced. You learn about the soft palate at the roof of your mouth, and that it must be raised when reaching for higher notes in your head voice. You think about how long you should sustain a note, or whether to use vibrato at the end of a phrase. I was always preoccupied with my own voice, its resonance and power. But I don't remember ever being taught to listen, at least not in the ways I was taught to express myself. It wasn't until I learned to sign that I came to grasp an error in our collective thinking—mouths are not prerequisites for speech any more than hearing is a prerequisite for listening.

Funnily enough, one of the first things you're taught as a beginner in Auslan is the sign for 'voice off': the knuckle of the index finger turned over at the throat as if locking a door. Deaf teachers and community members expect you to observe this request for silence. To slip into spoken language, rather than attempt to use sign, is considered rude. In order to step into the Deaf world, hearing people have to learn to shut up.

There's a powerful TED Talk, 'Navigating Deafness in a Hearing World', given by Rachel Kolb, a Deaf academic. In her presentation, she decides to use spoken English rather than American Sign Language. She could have used ASL, she explains, briefly signing and speaking at once. 'That would have been a perfectly viable choice.' She goes on to say, 'I'm starting this way because as a Deaf person there's many things I've been told I can't do, either by other people, or by that internal voice we all have.

'I've always known my speech isn't perfect,' she continues. 'Even now, oftentimes, I'll meet a person and they'll say: "I can't quite place your accent. Are you from England? Australia? Scandinavia?"' The audience laughs. And then she recounts an experience she had in middle school upon giving an oral presentation. In front of her peers, she stood up and delivered what she had practised. Afterwards, her teacher told her that she should never speak like that in front of a group without an interpreter present. 'It's not fair to anyone who has to listen to you.'

As I watched this video for the first time, it occurred to me that my grandmother likes to speak for this very same reason—because the world had told her she couldn't, and she was determined to prove them wrong. Where Grandpa was more at home with his hands, Nanny seems desperate at times to show others what she can do, what she has learned through years of hard-won practice. In many ways, she is the poster child for oralism, one of the lucky few for whom the method was a success. She thinks of speech as a gift, bestowed upon her by her teachers. Every time she opens her mouth, she summons her courage, and the lessons Miss Rhodes imparted.

But for Grandpa, whose foghorn expressions seemed imprisoned in my phone, I cannot locate him through audio alone. To appreciate him fully, I need visuals, for his voice was always carried in his hands.

10.

At the age of twenty-five, I enrolled in an Auslan course. When I told my grandfather about it, his eyebrows shot into his forehead. 'Why would you want to do that?' he asked.

Signing has long been a point of contention in my family. Depending on who you speak to, the claims and connected stories differ. There are gaps and silences in each—vast chunks of uncharted and volatile terrain.

My mother had hoped to raise us as bilingual, and at preschool I was praised for using my hands to speak. In my baby book, Mum recorded my first signs alongside my first words. In an uncanny coincidence, my first sign was 'pig'. When my brother was at preschool, he signed with ease. We have videos of his preschool Christmas concert, signing along emphatically to carols. But with Nanny and Grandpa, our adoption of the Deaf language was ambivalently received. Depending on the day, it was either tolerated or ignored, sometimes considered sweet. There were times it was unwelcome entirely.

I remember being small and out at the shops with Nanny. I signed something to her, and she waved my hands away. It was common for us kids to talk to Nanny and Grandpa with grandiose gestural flourishes. We enunciated and moved with zeal. I knew nothing then of my capacity to embarrass. Increasingly, I discerned the appropriate use of my 'indoor voice' and 'outdoor voice'—there were different rules for home and the outside world.

My mother would often lament my grandpa's resistance to signing with his grandchildren. She held him directly accountable for the slight, and given the opportunity, would speak at length of the grievance. The issue became more pressing in the years he was partially blind. He was never a great lipreader, but for years after the car accident he could barely follow the lips of anyone but Nanny. Frequently, she would backfill entire conversations for his benefit.

For my grandfather, dialogues were difficult, and produced in him a kind of resignation within hearing company. In large groups, he placed himself on the sidelines, eyes wandering around the room rather than watching conversations unfolding around him. When he had something to say, he'd deliver a monologue, unaware his interjections were poorly timed. He would wait for acknowledgement and then drift elsewhere as people resumed their chatter.

Some years ago, during dinner on a family holiday, an ex-boyfriend unwittingly grazed the surface of this familial tension. He asked how my mother learned to sign and was shocked when she revealed her late acquisition of the language. She picked it up when she began work in a Deaf school in 2009. Before then, her vocabulary was limited to a few basic signs. As he expressed polite interest in the topic, Mum poured forth her frustrations. 'I sent my kids to a signing preschool so they could communicate with *him*.' Grandpa caught my mother's eye, and she turned to address him directly. 'I tried to encourage you to sign to them, but you wouldn't have it. And without practice, well, it's all forgotten!'

Grandpa exhaled through tautened lips, turned his head, and proceeded to stare out the window. No matter how my mother banged the table and waved in his face, he would not entertain the conversation. Nanny wrung her hands and tried to soften the pair with affectionate rubs. For the rest of the evening, neither spoke a word.

For twenty-five years I had communicated verbally with my grandparents. I knew enough sign language to help with basic translation but not to hold an entire adult conversation. Up until then we'd been content with that arrangement. Nevertheless, my grandfather's reticence to encourage me came as a surprise. Perhaps he felt my newfound lingual interest abrupt. Perhaps intrusive.

Soon before my first lesson, and many months after the altercation with Mum, Grandpa confided in me. 'Your mother thinks I wouldn't sign to her, but that's not true,' he said. 'She told me once that she "understood my voice and I didn't need to sign".' He looked pained but shrugged his shoulders and said nothing more. I asked him how old my mother was at the time. She was thirteen.

In the subsequent days, I mused on the arcane power of a young girl's flippant remark. I thought of my grandmother as a child, enunciating before a mirror with chalk on her hands, and my grandfather, signing covertly in school dormitories while a comrade stood guard. I thought too of the weight of history, of hands being monitored for any disobedience. Back then, theirs was an underground language, used in hidden enclaves, reserved for trusted circles.

When Grandpa asked me why I wanted to sign, I gave a platitude about 'curiosity' and 'expanding my skill set'. Perhaps he intuited what I did not say. I wanted to communicate his way. No intermediary or fumbled clarifications. It's possible that in our hurried exchange, my grandfather was privy to my quest, to cross the murky borderlands between us and meet him on the other side.

•

My first Auslan lesson took place in a nameless building in Chatswood hired out by the Deaf Society of New South Wales. At the front of the room was a whiteboard with the words 'NO VOICE' printed in bold across the top. When the teacher arrived, rolling up the sleeves of her electric-blue shirt, she busied herself with papers and barely looked up to acknowledge the students filing in for the evening class.

After ten minutes of silence, she smiled and began a signed intro-duction. She told us her name: 'Margie', fingerspelling the letters with care. She said she was married to a man named Richard, had no children, and one dog. For a moment, I commended myself. I understood what she was saying!

Margie started to move faster and faster. She used more complex sentences and her fingerspelling was fluid. I fixated on her hands but received only snippets. Margie is hearing, not deaf. She grew up in . . . (where?). Now she lives in H_R _ _ Y (damn!). Husband—some-thing, something. Excited! Good—something, something NE _ _.

As she sped to the point I could no longer follow, my eyes darted around the room. There were students staring blankly ahead, mouths slightly agape. Others looked petrified and exchanged confused glances. Our teacher grinned and exhaled. Then she spoke out loud. 'Oh, thank god!' one woman exclaimed. 'I thought I was in the wrong room!'

Margie repeated her introduction, this time verbally. She explained that she worked as an interpreter and would be taking us for the first three classes. After that, we would have a Deaf teacher. Margie asked the class—all ten of us women—to consider how we felt during her signed preamble. One woman volunteered that she felt lost, stupid and alienated. She likened the experience to being in a foreign country. 'I felt like a stranger, but in my own city,' she said. Many others nodded and murmured their assent.

'Mmmm,' Margie said. 'It might give you a bit of an insight into how Deaf people can feel in the hearing world.' Lipreading what is often your second language isn't easy, and there is great variance in ability. Some deaf people don't lipread at all and find it tedious. 'On average, the message received is 30 per cent accurate,' she told us.

Research into lipreading shows that 50 per cent of English words are thought to be visually ambiguous. This is because of homophemes: words that sound different but involve identical movements of the speaker's lips. My grandmother had tried explaining this to me in the past. Words like 'white', 'wine', 'wide', or 'why' can all look the same, particularly if you're conversing with a lazy speaker. Words like 'dog', 'duck', and 'dark' are easily confused, and can cause strain for the reader. Context is often key but doesn't always provide everything.

Things like dim lighting, laughter, hand gestures and accents can make the process harder. In her short film, *Can You Read My Lips?*, Rachel Kolb explains this beautifully. 'The word lipreading implies reading like reading a book whose text is legible and clear,' she says. 'But the human face isn't a book, and lipreading isn't reading.' People mumble and talk quickly. They unknowingly cover their mouths or have 'facial hair like porcupines, lips like sphincters'. Lipreading is like putting together a puzzle with missing pieces, she says.

For the times that lipreading failed, fingerspelling was the best strategy. Because she never learned, my sister would occasionally struggle with Nanny and Grandpa. Overhearing the ways she'd repeat the same sentence over and over, I'd direct her from the sidelines. 'Try a synonym,' I'd say, and she'd glare at me.

'What?'

'A different word.'

When she repeated herself yet again, I'd grow impatient and march over to relay her meaning with my hands. Once the message was received, I'd walk away feeling her eyes on my back. I'm sure she'd have liked to thump me.

Even when my skills were at their most basic, I was too brazen for my own good. I inserted myself into dynamics I was not invited into. Watching conversations miscarry between Ray and Grandpa, I'd step in and interpret. Grandpa's eyes would flick between Ray and me, and though my uncle was gracious, and sometimes seemed grateful, I felt as though I'd trodden on toes.

There were times it was useful, or that I was recruited to help family members out of tricky spots. On occasion a voice would spring up from the quiet, usually my cousin Ben or my brother, James, sometimes even Auntie Ruth, to clarify their fingerspelling with me. 'What's G again?' or 'what's H?' and I'd demonstrate, leaving conversations to flow on smoothly behind me.

But on that first night of class, I was humbled. There was lots I did not know, and plenty I would learn. Sensing our shellshock, Margie encouraged her students not to worry. 'Signing is creating new muscle memory,' she said. 'It's like playing the piano. Your muscles get used it. After a while you won't have to think about it.'

We looked nothing like pianists that night. And for months we resembled infants, discovering our hands as if for the first time.

•

In the early stages of my learning, I had an obvious advantage over my peers, having previously had exposure to the language and to Deaf culture. For much of the time we discussed Deaf awareness, I was mouthy and forthright with my opinions. I finished the community courses and then moved on to certificate level. These were held onsite at the Deaf Society on Phillip Street, Parramatta. I grew fond of the unassuming classrooms and the neighbouring cafes where I'd go during study breaks and be greeted by staff members who had learned a few signs on account of their Deaf clientele.

With every class, I felt parts of myself awakening as though they'd been yanked from a hidden corner of my brain. In certificate level, all the teachers were Deaf and communicated with us by writing on the whiteboard. Sometimes the more timid classmates directed their questions to me, whispering them out of sight of our teacher. 'How do you say this, or that?' they'd ask. At first, I allowed myself to be flattered and gave the answer. Eventually it felt disrespectful. 'Ask the teacher,' I'd say.

Lessons were delivered in weekend blocks every month, where we'd sign after work on Friday and until evening on Saturdays and Sundays. As the content became more challenging, I felt myself being stretched. The fatigue could be punishing, and I often returned home in a state of cognitive and sensory overload. Concentrating in a second language—a visual one, no less—requires your undivided attention. Looking away means you miss vital information. There was no tuning out unless I was content to be in the dark.

Full-body immersion was non-negotiable, especially since Auslan contains two-handed signs and a two-handed alphabet. This is distinct from other languages like American Sign Language, which uses a one-handed alphabet. In juggling both hands, I was also navigating the four key elements of sign, described by Johnston and Schembri as 'Handshape, Orientation, Location and Movement'.

Auslan contains hundreds of distinct signs but is built out of sixty-two handshapes, thirty-seven of which form the core of the language, with the other twenty-five being non-significant variations of these. Each handshape can be oriented differently, directed either away from or towards the signer. Though I had a grasp of this before-hand, I began to discern patterns in the way these shapes get used, like the fact that the pinkie finger, perhaps purely coincidentally, is often used in signs conveying negative things: bad, worse, emerg-ency, devil, sick, rude.

'Location' of the sign refers to the sites of the body utilised in the meaning-making. The sign 'hungry', for example, is performed on the belly, while 'think' is located at the temple. The movement of signs varies too, as they journey from the body with different trajectories. In our introduction to linguistics, I learned that 'estab-lished signs'—signs that are fixed or frozen, highly standardised and most used—are different from 'productive signs', which are actively created by signers as they put together combinations of meaningful units. These are the signs often used in storytelling, created or re-created on the fly as required by the context to extend or modify the meaning of established signs.

Many of my classmates were surprised to learn that nations have their own unique sign language. Some of them wondered why there wasn't a single universal 'tongue'. But sign languages evolve much in the way that spoken languages do, descending from different parent languages and with much variation between them. Auslan has two main dialects: the southern dialect used in Victoria, South Australia, Western Australia and Tasmania, and the northern dialect used in New South Wales and Queensland. Signers from different regions can understand one another with ease, but occasionally, funny misunderstandings can arise. A colleague once told me about a trip she had taken to Melbourne with a group of deaf children from Sydney. The kids were horrified when a woman offered them cakes and used the southern sign for 'hungry'. In New South Wales, the action she performed—a thumb stroked twice across the side of the neck—means 'sex'.

Towards the end of the course, my class was taught about role shift, a key aspect of Auslan storytelling. This is where the signing body transitions from one character to another within a single story. We watched videos of one man telling elaborate tales and marvelled at the ways he contorted his limbs and face, easing seamlessly into different character positions. Our transitions were laboured and awkward. As we tried to inhabit the role of the second person in the narrative, we took steps to the side or pivoted abruptly at the shoulders. Our teachers were patient with our lack of subtlety. 'Try to think visually,' they encouraged. 'Show, don't tell.'

I had hungered for this knowledge, for the fine motor skills required to make stories spring from my limbs. But my artless impressions felt insultingly poor. At home, I practised in the mirror and recognised myself as the bumbling novice I was. My attempts conjured memories of high school drama class where we played improv games like 'space jump' and would be torn between doing our best and trying not to cringe.

In Auslan, everything is pictorial, and our teachers urged us to inject colour into our narratives. They reminded us about 'NMFs' or 'non-manual-features', which include facial expression and movements of the mouth, head and body. The use of stress, duration and repetition also fall under this umbrella. Often the manual and non-manual components occur simultaneously and can signal grammatical functions such as negation. For example, 'like' can be changed to 'dislike' through facial expression alone. Similarly, raising one's eyebrows can change a statement into a question.

Just as in spoken languages, signing requires discrimination in your choices. If you were telling a story about stumbling home from the pub, you might use the established sign for 'walk'—the index and middle fingers moved like legs across the flat surface of the palm—but modify it to resemble something akin to staggering. You'd do this by labouring the movement of the fingers, puffing air from your cheeks and swaying your head.

Putting these combinations together, I found myself absorbed by the choreography of Auslan phrasing. I practised compulsively. I signed in the shower, or as I walked down the street. Whenever I'd been drinking, I was suddenly hyper-eloquent, and often amused my Deaf friends by attempting to interpret song lyrics. This was a much bigger challenge, as English and Auslan aren't always commensurate.

Where English is usually linear with a fixed word order—subject, verb, object—Auslan is far more flexible. The verb clause can appear at sentence-initial, middle or sentence-final position and remain correct. Some English expressions don't translate well into Auslan either, particularly idioms like 'cat's got your tongue' or 'rule of thumb'. It works the other way, too. There are signs that don't have direct equivalents in English like 'ba-ba', a sign that gets its name from the mouth pattern associated with it and roughly translates to 'bizarre'. A signer will turn their hands out as though reaching to lift up a child, before rocking their hands twice from the wrist.

As I became more and more adept, signing almost habitually, Nanny and Grandpa began to defrost. At first, when I signed to them at home, Nanny scowled and said, 'I can lipread, you know.' Grandpa said nothing about it for some months, even though our conversations were much quicker, smoother than before. After a while, they started inviting me along to visit their Deaf friends, and sending me text messages when they intended on having visitors and could show me off in company.

One day, when I was in the middle of signing a story, my face becoming more and more theatrical, Nanny erupted into laughter. 'She's going Deaf!' she exclaimed to Grandpa. 'Just look at her.'

It wasn't until one of my grandfather's hospital stints that I realised what my new competence meant to him. As he lay in bed and I translated the instructions of doctors and nurses that flitted in and out of the room, a voice piped up from across the way. A fellow patient started a conversation with Grandpa. 'Your grand-daughter takes wonderful care of you,' he said, and Grandpa made the sign for 'what?' I relayed the man's message and Grandpa smiled. 'Yes,' he said. 'She's learned to sign just for me. It's wonderful.'

A little while after that hospital stay, one of their friends gave me my sign-name. These help to identify people quickly without needing to fingerspell, and mark your entrance into the community. They can only be given to you by a Deaf person. Mine is the American sign for 'J' followed by the sign for 'smile'. I found out later from a Deaf teacher that this is a little generic. But I didn't care. It was mine.

On the day I received it, I called my mother and gushed down the phone. She laughed at me. 'It's a bit like being christened, isn't it?' Later that night when I walked around the Sydney waterfront with friends, we passed the entrance to Luna Park. I looked up at the giant, strange mouth, with the ridiculous, almost maniacal grin of the clown face, and while my friends weren't watching, I prac-tised my new name to myself.

On the final day of my course, the class sat in a circle and took turns sharing the highlights of the Auslan experience. The outpouring of sentiment moved me, as did the ways that people felt 'transformed'. Some mentioned the ways they'd grown and had their perceptions changed. Others said they'd developed a deep love for the Deaf community.

Auslan classes inverted the order of the world. Within them, our teachers were powerful, knowledgeable figures and we regarded them with a kind of reverence. In their presence we became groupies, and they, our gurus. As part of our training, we attended Deaf social events and an 'Auslan Only Weekend', AOW, where you 'voice off' for the full duration of the camp. These events are striking for the ways they allow you to see Deaf people in their element—surrounded by peers, chatting furiously. I made many of my dearest friendships at AOWs.

By the end of my courses, I was wary of things I had seen in my classmates. I rolled my eyes at the over-eager few who had suddenly 'forgotten' that they were hearing. Some of them pretended to be deaf when out in public—an act considered culturally insensitive at best—and others developed a clumsy self-importance through their newfound role as an ally. I understood the righteous anger, the desire to soapbox. In my grandparents' defence, I could become a bulldog.

Nevertheless, I found myself contemplating allyship in new and challenging ways. With Nanny and Grandpa, I had developed a well-honed watchfulness, hovering on the sidelines should I be needed or asked for help. But with Deaf peers I found myself in a tangle of uncertainty. There were occasions where helping amounted to interfering. Sometimes the line was clear: being asked to interpret was one thing, but volunteering oneself was another. There are many stories of Auslan students encountering Deaf people in the world and interpreting without being asked. No doubt the impulse comes from a noble place, but is often received as a kind of 'speaking for' or 'speaking over'.

I was all the more conscious of these behaviours as I began to write this book. Mine was a complex inheritance of family knowledge and woeful ignorance, of understanding with an endpoint. When a Deaf scholar read an early draft of my writing, she noticed the ways I held back, pontificated and needlessly tiptoed. She urged me to be confident as I began to rewrite. I lost many nights of sleep contemplating how to give balance to the voices on the page. Had it not been for Nanny and Grandpa's input and encouragement, I might have given up entirely.

The issue of who should speak and who should listen becomes more pressing given the ways that Deaf people have fought for their own independence—for the right to manage their own affairs. For much of the twentieth century, Deaf organisations were run by hearing people who made executive decisions on their behalf. For decades, the Deaf community challenged the charity model of service provision and resisted controls imposed upon them. They pushed for greater agency and for Deaf leadership. Hearing interference can, understandably, be an affront to Deaf people's desire for self-determination.

And yet, the Deaf community is unmistakeably warm and enveloping. It can be a haven for many a misfit who enters and finds themselves at home. Newcomers and fringe-dwellers like me are often taken aback by the openness of the Deaf, how accepting and accommodating they can be.

For my entire life, my grandparents accommodated me. They made concessions when I forgot signs, they slowed down for me, or excused me if I was lazy and wanted to use my voice. But in class, no such concessions were made. In plunging myself deeper into the Deaf world I found myself confronting, as if for the first time, my own hearing identity.

Deaf Studies scholar Dirksen Bauman writes about the distinction between being a person who can hear and being *hearing*. The former is a biological fact, the latter is a social construction. He explains that his once-taken-for-granted or common-sense understanding of his hearingness unravelled when he got a job at a school for the deaf. 'Growing up,' he says, 'the thought that I was a hearing person had never crossed my mind; hearing was so normal it went unnoticed. It was just the way things were. I became *hearing* at the age of twenty-one. Suddenly, my world changed: it was no longer *my* world.'

In a similar way, I became hearing in my time at the Deaf Society. Somehow, through the process of looking out at deafness, I was faced with myself.

•

It's not only my grandparents who have been ambivalent about Auslan. My sister and I have disagreed over its use. Once, as I signed something to Nanny and Grandpa, Lizzie looked at me and said, 'Do they really understand all that?' My face gave her the answer, and she backed away, shrugging her shoulders. But perhaps the biggest blow, one I never mentioned to my grandparents, came a few years ago at the dinner table.

My father was cooking us a meal, and Mum was weaving in and out of the room, putting away washing and tidying up. I was playing with my niece. Back when she was little, I used to babysit while my sister went to work. I often sang to her and included signs for her to copy. After a while, she began repeating them back to me and I'd clap and cheer. I never thought much of these activities, only that I was arming her with language, that signing might be another tool in her linguistic belt. Perhaps, too, she could use it to communicate with her great-grandparents. My sister was otherwise grateful for initiatives I took with my niece: reading to her, teaching her words, colours and numbers. But signing, I soon found, was not welcome.

As I waited for dinner, I signed something to Zara and my sister exploded.

'Why are you signing to her?' she demanded, furious. 'She's not deaf! I don't want her walking around like this.' She began flapping her arms wildly about the room. Her face was contorted into stupefaction.

I asked her if she was joking. 'No,' she shot back. 'I don't want her doing that. It doesn't look good.' I scoffed, reminding her that her grandparents were deaf, and did she have any idea how offensive—? But my father cut me off.

'You're not the parent here, Jessica,' he said. 'It's Lizzie's choice.'

He was right, but I couldn't stand it.

Later that night I wailed to Mum about my sister's insensitivity, thinking she'd overheard the disagreement. 'Why didn't you say anything?' I demanded. Mum looked blankly at me. She was out of the room when it happened and must've re-entered when she heard our voices raised. Without pause, I recounted the entire conversation, stressing the parts I found most enraging, and watched my mother's face fall.

I doubt my sister would respond the same way now. Auslan is more visible, trendy even. In 2020, for example, Deaf Connect reported a 400 per cent increase in their enrolments in online Auslan classes because of the increased use of sign language in Covid broadcasts. A national curriculum was developed for Auslan in 2016, and from March 2023, students in NSW schools will have the option to provide Auslan classes from kindergarten to grade ten. In the last few years, teachers have been taking more initiatives to bring Auslan into classrooms. About a year ago, Zara came home from school having been shown how to sign 'I Can Sing a Rainbow'. When she performed it to us all, Lizzie smiled and nothing was said about her past reservations. Perhaps she had feared for Zara being ostracised and figured that if everyone was doing it now, she wouldn't be teased.

There are times that I ache for my mother, knowing how she's toiled to support and appease her parents. But daughterly work is often thankless, expected and invisible. All her best intentions—her efforts to connect and keep us all involved in Nanny and Grandpa's world—and yet she often felt discouraged. Grandpa changed his tune too late for her, and though she was never begrudging, I am the one who reaped the benefits of everything Mum had tried in years gone by. She had to fight for the things I won with relative ease.

Not long into my lessons, my signing skills overtook hers, and there were times I wanted to squash myself, to take up less space. I knew my mother was proud of me; she frequently told me so. She encouraged me to keep studying and to consider a career in interpreting. But somehow, guilt lodged in my stomach like concrete.

One day, as I volunteered at the school my mum once worked in, an ex-colleague of hers complimented my signing. 'You're better than your mum,' she said, 'bless her.' She slapped a hand to her mouth then and admonished herself. 'Gosh, I'm being terrible,' she continued. 'Your mum is absolutely wonderful, but signing isn't her forte.'

Her limitations weren't for a lack of trying. On the eve of Nanny and Grandpa's fortieth wedding anniversary, when I was about ten, my mother gave a speech in Auslan. She had a Deaf friend of the family teach her and practised it over and over before delivering it to a room full of Deaf people. Perhaps Grandpa appreciated it and was proud of her then, but he never let on.

There were many things my grandfather left unsaid, both in words and signs. He was a tender man, but like many of his generation, he kept his feelings close to his chest. On Grandpa's eighty-sixth birthday, Mum baked a cake and the family gathered round to sing him happy birthday. We stood in a half-moon shape around him, with my mother at one end, and me at the other. As everyone else sang, Mum and I signed the lyrics.

But Grandpa could not hold us both in his sights at once. He was looking at me, blushing, laughing, shoulders scrunched at his ears. My mother watched on as he glowed, observing, in a single moment, all the things she desired but could not have for herself.

11.

My mother learned to drive in a green Vauxhall Viva with her father at her side. From the passenger seat, he used to edge forward in his chair as though willing the vehicle onwards. It sent her mad. Whenever they drove together, he gave instructions that were useless to a hearing person. 'Go this way,' he'd say, pointing in the direction he meant. But Mum was too busy scanning the road for oncoming traffic and could not see his hands. 'Which way?' she'd ask, and Grandpa would merely repeat his previous action. 'Use words!' she would plead. 'Left or right?' and Grandpa would throw his hands in the air and lose his temper. My grandfather found it hard to give instruction or explain in English what needed to be done. 'He was like an alarm bell,' my mum explained, 'but you never knew what the issue was.'

Once, as they approached the crest of a hill, my mother stalled the car. She didn't know how to do a hill start, and as the transmission cut out, she froze. 'Porhhhhhhh!' Grandpa wailed, shaking his head furiously. Mum fled the car, slamming the door behind her, and stormed off in the direction of their home. After Grandpa reinstalled himself at the wheel, he trailed behind her, flinging the door open when he caught up, a wordless instruction to 'get in'.

My mother is a CODA, or a 'child of deaf adult'. In the Deaf world this acronym distinguishes an identity category, a subset of the community that are, culturally speaking, neither hearing nor deaf but somewhere in between. The term generally applies to the hearing children of d/Deaf parents: children who are raised with the ways of the deaf but are part of the dominant hearing culture.

CODAs often occupy a precarious position, straddling the margins of both worlds and acting as an interpreter and conduit for their parents. At an early age they negotiate the adult world and take on responsibilities that are foreign to other children. When my mother was a child, she had to interpret Nanny and Grandpa's medical appointments and make phone calls on their behalf. She remembers the first call she ever placed at the age of seven, when Nanny led her to a public pay phone and expected that Mum would know what to do.

Making social arrangements was all right, but other calls were taxing. The more formal ones to doctors or other professionals were often difficult to navigate. Sometimes there were grown-up things my mum couldn't understand, but she recognised her privileged position. She knew she was one step ahead of her parents, simply because she could hear. Other times her duties left her anxious, particularly when working against the constraints of the payphone system. You only had a limited amount of time before the phone would start beeping, signalling the need to insert another tenpence. My mother learned to be succinct, but sometimes Nanny ran out of coins and the call would get cut off.

It took finesse to balance the pleasantries and flow of hearing conversation against the desires of Nanny and Grandpa to be active participants in their own affairs. Sometimes everyone would talk at once. Nanny and Grandpa would want to know what was being said, and always insisted you face them so they could lipread one half of the conversation. But often they jumped in when Mum was listening to pertinent information. The interjections came in bursts: 'What did they say?' 'Make sure you tell them . . .' 'Can you ask them . . . ?'

During my mother's adult life, her responsibilities persisted and us kids would be enlisted to help. I didn't take my role as a GODA—grandchild of deaf adult—lightly.

I often filled in for Mum when she wasn't around or when Uncle Ray and Auntie Ruth weren't available. In later years when passwords and identity checks were required by telecommunications companies, I often had to endure the rigmarole of authorising consent. I would explain the situation to the person on the other end of the line, who would then apologise and insist they couldn't speak to you unless you were the account holder. Then I would have to pass the phone to Grandpa, because his speech was clearest, and he would yell down the phone, giving me verbal permission to do his bidding.

Nanny and Grandpa were mindful and made every effort to offset the potential strain placed upon their two children. Where possible they functioned independently, booking their appointments with the hairdresser or mechanic in person and well in advance. But sometimes things came up at the last minute, and the world was not set up to accommodate them. Doctors' surgeries presented a challenge in that they used a ticketing system where you'd be given a number and asked to wait until yours was called. Nanny would be on edge as she sat there with Mum, checking incessantly which number was last announced.

There is a type of intimacy forged in having unmitigated access to your parents' lives, and my mother didn't resent her role. When I asked her about it, she said it felt like an honour, and a way of getting their approval. Nanny and Grandpa were so grateful. They thanked and praised her for her cleverness. Small feats were met with such celebration, and she knew that mostly she could pull things off. There were occasions, though, where she craved a break. Even at home, she was constantly alert. 'People would knock on the door and my antennae would go up,' she told me, as I asked her what it was like for her. 'I was always hanging in the background, waiting to be called to the fore.' The only place she could be a child was at her parents' Deaf club, where she was no longer needed. 'It was like time off,' she said.

There have been times too where such intimacy has been uncomfortable. In hospitals and specialist rooms, Mum has been required to ask her parents about their sex life, or their bowel and bladder movements, and relay their answers to the medical staff taking care of them.

When Nanny speaks of my mother as a child, she remarks on how capable she was. She learned so quickly, took to language like a sponge. Though my grandparents signed to one another at home, they always addressed my mother in spoken English. From the earliest age, they surrounded her with words and sounds. In his barrelling deaf voice, my grandfather recited verse as she sat on his lap, and Nanny spent her afternoons teaching Mum to read and write. Once the children's programs had finished on television, they'd sit together and pore over the Ladybird reading series, Peter and Jane. Nanny read aloud and Mum would follow along.

Though nobody ever corrected her speech, Mum was sensitive to issues of diction and elocution, knowing her parents weren't the authority on such matters. She found herself listening closely to the ways that hearing people spoke, how words were pronounced and sentences composed. My grandparents made slight errors at times, said things that didn't sound quite right. Place names and words containing 'ng' were especially hard, and occasionally Nanny missed syllables in words like 'yoghurt', where she dropped the 'g' altogether.

Gently, Mum would point out the mistakes. Nanny would thank her and say it was important that she knew. Grandpa rarely misspoke. He had a memory of sound, after all. But on the occasions he did, he'd shake his head, not cross with her for telling him, but disappointed that he'd forgotten himself.

When Mum and my uncle were infants, Nanny and Grandpa had a baby monitor with a wire that coiled around the slats of the cot and measured sound waves. Whenever they would cry, a light would flash beside the bed, and Nanny would wake and attend to them. Before such technology existed, deaf parents were resourceful. I've heard stories of mothers tying string to their baby's ankle and then to their own wrist, so if the child threw their limbs about as they wailed, they'd be alerted to the motion.

But however tethered deaf parents are to their children, there's a tension that exists between them. There's an Australian documentary called *Passport Without a Country*, which my mum watched in the early 1990s. It was one of the first to give voice to her experiences. She knew many of the people interviewed and could relate to the things they shared on camera. In the opening scenes, one man articulates the duality and struggle of the CODA experience. 'Because our ears work,' he says, 'you can't get too involved in some of the political things that Deaf people are trying to achieve for themselves. That hurts because it feels like they're saying you don't belong.'

Another explains his closeness and separateness from deafness. 'It's like having a passport,' he says. 'You belong to that country but that passport is never recognised by the authorities. It won't admit you into that world, although you've got it, and it was given to you by birth.' As he speaks, he begins to cry, sharing his decision to remove himself entirely from the community. 'But every now and then,' he concedes, 'I feel the need to talk in sign language.'

'It's me,' he says. 'I'm neither one nor the other. I don't know what I am.'

Around the same time the film was released, a support group for CODAs was launched in the New South Wales State Library. There are now many of its kind all around the world. The groups often meet socially and hold conferences for members, aiming to speak to the shared experience of feeling Deaf at heart but hearing in body.

When Mum found out about the launch, she offered to bring Nanny and Grandpa along. The three of them attended together, and there were both Deaf and hearing people in the room that night. When my mother recounted the events that unfolded, she said that the presenters were measured and thoughtful. There was much affection for Deaf culture in the room, and most of the problems raised were those relating to the cruelty of hearing people. A common refrain was the need to address the ways that CODAs overheard and then internalised the taunts of others.

But when Grandpa told me about that evening, he did so through gritted teeth.

'CODAs are always moaning,' he said, grimacing. He said that people at the event stood up and gave accounts of their lives. One of them complained that as a child he'd wanted a glass of water in the night but could not cry out to ask for it. Grandpa parodied the man's performance. He made the sign for 'thirsty'—a finger running down his throat—before rolling his eyes.

'We're not with them,' Grandpa said. 'They just get together to whinge about their parents. That's all.'

·

My mother has never seemed to belong anywhere; at least, not to any place I knew of. She was at home within our family, but in my mind, she was a hybrid creature: an Englishwoman with a love of the Australian climate and an accent that shifted with her company. There was a statelessness about her, a restlessness and indecisiveness I found curious. She often played with ideas about living by the sea, or maybe a river, or buying an apartment in the city. As a child I was dragged to open homes down the coast, or in the bush, or to whichever fanciful place my mother's mind had entertained in the months prior.

She had a rich work life, was highly competent, driven, and extremely likeable, with the warmth of her mother and the wit of her father. Nonetheless, her identity was always relational: something she carried on in her approach to mothering. My brother once remarked on our mother's capacity for empathy. He felt that in his every endeavour, Mum had felt his wins and losses acutely. I think perhaps with her children as well as her parents, it was hard to distinguish where they ended and she began.

In the days after I was born, my mother performed her own hearing tests on me, being familiar with the methods her colleagues used. It was unlikely I would be deaf. As far as we know there's no genetic predisposition to deafness in our family, as both Nanny and Grandpa went deaf through sudden illness. But for Mum, it felt a possibility, however slim. When the two of us were alone, she laid me on the hospital bed and knocked against various surfaces, waiting to see if I'd react. She held her breath and then exhaled as she watched my eyes go still at the sound. Though she was prepared and well-positioned to raise a deaf child, she was glad I was hearing. Not because she saw deafness as something terrible or pitiful, but because she knew the inhospitality of the hearing world.

By the time the next generation of our family came along, there was no suggestion of deafness at all. My two nieces, Zara and Imogen, passed their newborn infant screening without issue. But on the day after Immi was born, I had one of the biggest fights with my mum I've ever had.

Where I am my mother's daughter—emotive and tactile—my sister, Lizzie, is more like my father: stoic and harder at the surface. When she asked both Mum and me to be present at the birth, we were thrilled. In the delivery room, I sat with my sister and held her hands during the epidural. The crowns of our heads were touching, my dark brown locks set against her platinum blonde. Midway through the procedure, Mum came into the room with takeaway coffees. Lizzie looked up at me, panicked. 'Tell her to come back later,' she said, wanting to avoid our mother fussing over her. I nodded and waved Mum away, watching her face fall as she disappeared behind a curtain.

In the minutes before Imogen was born, we fumbled with cameras and video calls to my sister's partner, who was overseas and unable to get home. The midwife had been yelling at us: 'She's crowning! Quick! You're going to miss it.' I snatched the phone from Mum's hands and chided her for faffing about. The next day, I felt the weight of what I'd done.

We stood on the driveway of my sister's house, swapping shifts on the child-minding schedule we'd arranged for my eldest niece. While she was inside packing her things, we argued beside the car, hissing at one another through tears. My mother told me I had muscled in and taken charge. I had forgotten about her, usurped her position. I had been overzealous, and she said I was often the same with Nanny and Grandpa, that I frequently took over and managed to push her out. I was wounded. I told her that I only had good intentions. In both scenarios I was just trying to be helpful, and besides, I said, 'I wonder where I learned that behaviour?'

My mother was silent for a moment. She reflected on her own propensity for micro-managing. 'Maybe,' she said slowly, almost sheepishly, 'it's just difficult for me because you often have better ideas than I do.'

I'm not sure why I felt it was my place to write the story of my mother's parents. Perhaps it was because I am the eldest grandchild, and that whether through accident or design, I have spent the most amount of time with them. Maybe, too, I've always felt an intrinsic connection with Nanny and Grandpa, something instilled in me from their tales about the past.

My grandmother often tells me about the day my sister was born. I was twenty months old, and Nanny and Grandpa were minding me while my parents were in the hospital. While we were together, the phone rang. It was my mother calling to announce Lizzie's arrival. I answered the phone and told Nanny and Grandpa that I had a new baby sister. In every telling of this tale, Nanny marvels at how instinctively I rushed to the phone, holding it against my ear and then pausing to transmit the incoming message. I was so grown up. Clever, like my mother. 'You knew we were deaf,' she says. 'Somehow, you just understood.'

It's not surprising to me now that Mum and I clashed as much as we did that day. But what my mother does not know is the enormousness of the shoes I'm attempting to fill. Perhaps she's unaware that sometimes Nanny and Grandpa would accidentally call me by her name, little slippages that speak of how we've been held alongside one another in their hearts. I look a lot like her, and sometimes when we're together people will remark on the overlaps in our mannerisms and facial features.

It's almost unthinkable, much less speakable, but I have wondered about what my mother's life would have been like if her parents were hearing. Perhaps she's wondered the same thing herself. It's impossible to disentangle my grandparents from their deafness, much as it might be to separate my own identity from womanhood, say, or whiteness. Our lives with Nanny and Grandpa were so enmeshed that I can barely imagine life otherwise. Sharing a home with Nanny and Grandpa came with its difficulties, but it felt safer having them close, especially as they grew older and less independent.

When Grandpa died, my mother made all the arrangements. Nobody questioned it. But there's a paradox in the ways my mother relates to her parents: that a lack of boundaries, in some respects, has led to a life being bound to them. Her years of service were driven by a fierce and urgent devotion. Might she have known another way, were the world more attuned to the ones she loved?

12.

My grandparents fell in love in the spring of 1958. They met at a Deaf dinner-dance held at the Wolverhampton Civic Hall, a thickset building fronted by a grand stone facade. Inside the Wulfrun Hall— the room booked for the event—the tables were draped with white linen and arranged in a horseshoe configuration so everyone could see and sign to one another. There was a ballroom dancefloor and a big band played on an elevated stage. The music was loud. Guests could feel the vibrations through the wooden floorboards.

It was an annual event held by the Midlands Deaf Sports Association (MDSA), where people from all the different Deaf clubs in the region—Birmingham, Wolverhampton, Derby, Coventry and Stoke—would join together. When my grandparents were young, every town in England had a Deaf club and it was common to have membership in several at once, in order to meet more people. Generally, though, you spent most of your time at whichever centre was local. Grandpa belonged to Wolverhampton, and Nanny to Birmingham, neighbouring but distinct metropolitan boroughs.

Individual clubs threw their own events: bingo nights, card nights, lectures, fundraisers, plays, group outings and performances by travelling Deaf comedians. Throughout the year, the MDSA ran indoor sporting tournaments, and the clubs used to compete against each other in games like billiards and darts. They played home and away games all over the Midlands. Once a year came the dinner-dance, an opportunity to mix with a much bigger crowd.

Nanny hadn't planned to attend, but a friend had pleaded with her. This friend was going to be set up on a blind date that night and wanted someone to come along in case the guy was a dud. So, Nanny went. She wore a cocktail dress and her most elegant heels. My grandmother did her duty at first, hovering beside her friend as she chatted with her date. But the couple soon disappeared somewhere, and Nanny was left alone at the table. As she looked out to the dancefloor, a tall man approached her. The man's name was Melvyn Hunt, and she would marry him less than a year later.

Many hearing people are shocked when I mention that both my grandparents are deaf. When they learn that two deaf people have spent their lives together, they seem touched, and sometimes they'll say how lucky they must've been to find one another. But my grandparents' relationship is far from novel. More often than not, Deaf people end up together. In fact, the Deaf world has the highest rate of intermarriages of any cultural or linguistic group. In the United States, for example, 85 per cent of people with profound deafness will marry another deaf person.

This rate is unsurprising given the ways the Deaf world is structured. Deaf people talk about Deaf ethnicity or 'Deafnicity' as a defining feature of their collective identity. In citing their shared language, culture, institutions, sense of belonging and kinship, they often suggest their experiences of marginalisation are analogous to other minority groups. In matters of romance, this has typically meant that Deaf people expect and encourage Deaf partnerships, and sometimes regard relationships between Deaf and hearing people with scepticism on account of linguistic and cultural barriers. Dating deaf–deaf means an even playing field. There's no need to explain or defend Deaf culture, or to learn new modes of communication and understanding.

When I asked my grandparents to tell me the story of how they met, Nanny took the lead. While she steered me through the sequence of events, Grandpa sat in the armchair beside her and blushed, occasionally offering up odd tidbits about his two left feet or the threepence annual membership fee for his Deaf club. As they spoke, it became clear that my grandparents' tale was as much about them as a couple as it was about their community. So interwoven were their love and the clubs they belonged to that remnants of each were often uttered in the same breath.

Pulling out the photo albums, Nanny and Grandpa showed me pictures of various outings and events they attended in their youth. Most were taken with the Midlands Deaf Club, a private club where Nanny had been secretary and actively involved in organising events. Nanny spoke of this with her nose held slightly in the air, as though their participation here was somehow prestigious, more dignified. She placed emphasis on the word 'private', forming the sign as she spoke it aloud: hand erect like a fin and drawn towards the chin, the rim of the fingers placed gently below the lips.

I was ready to chide my grandmother's snobbery. But unlike the public groups with their missioners and welfare workers who worked with the church, this club was run entirely by Deaf people. In those days, many Deaf clubs had active involvement from the Church of England and missioners were central figures in the community. This meant that hearing people controlled and influenced much of Deaf life. It was a powerful move to be independent, to strike out on their own.

Nanny took pride in her duties: booking coaches, counting the small change in the kitty, taking minutes and records of the committee meetings. Sometimes she was even the Master of Ceremonies at their functions. In the months of their engagement Grandpa joined the club, where they met every second Saturday of the month, hiring a room in Livery Street in Birmingham, right near the Snow Hill train station.

When the private group dissolved, they went back to Wolverhampton Deaf Club in Rupert Street: a landmark centre for the community. In many ways the building was unremarkable. It was a redbrick Edwardian home converted to serve the purposes of the club. It had white single-hung windows and a dark hip-roof without an eave, all of which combined to make its face appear featureless and cleanshaven. When you'd open the front door and walk down the hall, you eventually came to a living area: an enormous games room with a television and dartboards fixed to the walls. There was a snooker table and table tennis, and chairs scattered round so people could drag them together and chat.

Between the big room and the kitchen there was a hole in the wall for food to be passed through. People would eat on their laps, resting plates on their knees while their hands busied themselves in conversation. Thursday and Saturday nights were most popular, and on Sunday they ran a Deaf church service from the chapel upstairs. My mother can remember Christmas parties here, where she watched the adults engrossed in their activities, all the hands and faces in motion before her.

My grandparents told of a bygone era: the halcyon days of the community when they attended black tie events in London, five-course dinners in Coventry with special acts, performances from pantomime actors and acrobats. 'Most of the clubs are gone now,' Nanny told me. 'Finished, or they've gotten smaller.' She made the sign for 'less': two hands drawing nearer and nearer to one another until they almost touch. 'Times have changed, that's all,' Grandpa echoed.

This change has taken place all over the world. In the United States and Europe, Deaf clubs have experienced dramatic decline. After a period of rapid expansion and popularity, the 1970s and '80s saw a complete reversal of the trend, with many clubs collapsing. Of the few that are left now, membership is small and elderly.

Historian Carol Padden cites a range of social and economic factors that may have led to the disappearance of brick-and-mortar places for Deaf communities. Changes in communication technology like closed captioning in television, video and DVD players; the internet and online spaces are all offered up as contributing factors that may have kept people at home. Others speculate about widespread contemporary practices like placing deaf children in mainstream schools and the popularity of cochlear impacts as other related and potentially detrimental shifts. The cultural push for 'inclusion', though well-intended, has meant that the Deaf community, however resilient, is one under threat. It has also meant that many deaf kids end up isolated and lonely. Kept apart from others like them, many rush to the Deaf community later in life, hungry for acceptance and fellow feeling.

The Rupert Street Centre was closed in 2014. Its remaining members still gather, but not in the same way. Social networks are now mostly itinerant, moving from venue to venue. In Sydney, too, the Deaf community has seen many changes. Perhaps the biggest of these was the relocation of the Deaf Society of NSW to Parramatta in 1995 from its previous home in Stanmore. The Stanmore Deaf

Centre was a second home to many Deaf people in Sydney, much like Wolverhampton was for Nanny and Grandpa. There have been other closures too, of clubs and community initiatives. My grandparents can remember a thriving Sydney Deaf club in Burwood; today it has closed down entirely.

Hearing people familiar with the Deaf community often speak of 'Deaf-time' that stretches into infinity, where conversations and farewells are drawn out and extravagant. When I host parties, my Deaf guests are always the last to leave, and when I attend theirs, they're livelier, rowdier than those of my hearing friends. The dancing, drinking and socialising carries on until the early hours of the morning.

I imagine my grandparents absorbed in Deaf-time when they met. They danced together that evening, monitoring the beat through the vibrations that travelled through their feet and into their limbs. Though Nanny knew all the steps, Grandpa was unsteady and kept treading on her feet. His balance was always poor as a result of his meningitis as a child, so my grandmother steered him back to the table where they talked for the rest of the evening.

When they parted ways and he made no mention of seeing her again, Nanny was disappointed. She stayed overnight with her friend at the house of the Missioner for the Deaf. At eight o'clock the next morning, there was a knock at the door. Grandpa was outside, having learned of her whereabouts through friends. He wanted to know if she would spend the day with him.

The two set off in his car and drove around Wolverhampton. In the evening he put her on a train back home to Birmingham, waving goodbye at the platform, once again with no further plans to meet. The following Wednesday, Nanny played tennis in Hall Green with a friend. She was about to serve when the pair caught sight of my grandfather walking towards them. Nanny was surprised to see him and flattered when she learned he'd gone looking for her after sourcing her home address. My great-grandmother directed him to the tennis courts and, when Nanny returned that evening, spoke warmly of the young man who appeared on their doorstep. 'I like this one,' her mum had said. 'He's a good man.'

'We've been together ever since,' Nanny said, referring to that Wednesday afternoon. When they were married on the day of my grandpa's birthday in February 1959, he was twenty-six, and she was twenty-four. They were surrounded by their families, but also by a throng of Deaf peers—people they'd met from their Deaf schools and various Deaf clubs.

The group wedding photograph, taken outside St Agnes Church in Moseley, shows my grandparents standing tall in the centre of the image; my grandfather has a carnation pinned to his lapel, and my grandmother is in a long-sleeved white dress cinched in at the waist. Over her short curls, a veil is secured by a floral headpiece. On either side of them are their guests, as many Deaf friends as there are hearing family members.

When my grandparents first came to Australia, they left behind a robust circle of friendships they had honed over a lifetime. In Deaf circles, where you went to school is paramount. It functions as a marker of your Deaf identity, your history, and even your Deaf philosophy. The clubs you are part of, too, secure you a name and a place within a social hierarchy. The people in this new country weren't familiar with their schools, or their clubs. All of their time-honoured connections, their shared jokes and memories, the social roles and prestige they had accrued were not transferable to the Australian context. They soon found community in Sydney but needed to start over, build themselves from scratch.

My grandparents were dedicated to one another for sixty years. Our family celebrated the milestone anniversary while Grandpa was in the rehab clinic. In other centuries their union might have been threatened by the clout of eugenicists who opposed the inter-marriage of Deaf people. Among them, Alexander Graham Bell, who had a deaf wife himself, feared the creation of a deaf race as a result of these marriages. In his paper 'Memoir Upon the Formation of a Deaf Variety of the Human Race', which he presented to the National Academy of Sciences in 1883, he wrote that 'the production of a defective race of human beings would be a great calamity to the world', and advocated for deaf–hearing marriages to breed out the scourge of deafness.

Deaf people, both then and now, objected to this and responded in kind. In an article in *Science* magazine dated 30 January 1891, one deaf woman cursed the arrogance of 'learned men who think they know just what is proper for us, and would legislate us into marriage with hearing persons, and rob us of more domestic happiness than their theories would secure us in a thousand years'.

When Grandpa died, so did my grandmother's world. Her grief was piercing. On the day we lay Grandpa's ashes to rest, interring them in the earth, Nanny clutched at the mahogany box he was placed in at the crematorium. Before the minister arrived, we each took a turn holding it, saying our farewells. As we did so, Nanny grew impatient and snatched it from my arms. 'My Melvyn,' she said. 'He's mine.'

In those first weeks without him, the house was full of flowers, many sent from England. For a time, visitors popped in and then tapered off. Mum developed a nightly ritual of inviting Nanny in for a glass of wine, and I spent many nights in the spare room to keep my grandmother company. But it was never enough. She'd lost her primary ally, and though we were family, we just weren't the same. We never could be.

I once asked my grandparents about their ideal world. What would they envision for Deaf people of the future? Nanny spoke about unity and 'blending'. 'I want the hearing world to blend with the Deaf, and I want the Deaf world to blend with the hearing,' she said. 'It has to be both ways, from both directions.'

Grandpa was reticent. 'I don't know that it's possible,' he said with a frown. 'Have you heard the expression "Birds of a feather flock together"?' he asked. I nodded. He made the sign for 'deaf', followed by 'group', placing his hands at one end of the signing space. Then he made the sign for 'hearing', placing them on the opposite side. 'See?' he said, throwing his hands in the air. Nanny clucked her tongue and swatted him from the couch.

'Ooh, you're terrible,' she said, and Grandpa laughed. While my grandmother fawned over me, rambling about exceptions to the rule—especially family members who were 'in-between' and ever so important—Grandpa looked at the floor. He backtracked a little, nodding at Nanny's sentiment. Though he reached over to squeeze my arms, I knew that he thought what he thought, and there was no changing it.

13.

My grandmother has the hands of a child. Excepting the creases and wrinkles of her skin, the slight angulation of her arthritic fingertips, they are as soft and dimpled as an infant's. Nanny has thick, spatulate fingers, a cushiony palm and a broad wrist. Her fingernails are hewn right to the dorsal edge of the nailbed. Hers are busy, boisterous hands that accompany and animate her speech. They punctuate her sentences, sometimes filling in blanks where words don't suffice.

If Nanny thinks I look nice, she will give a compliment by way of pantomime. She will pose like a 1940s pin-up girl, thrusting a hip to one side, primping her hair, flicking her thumbs out over her waist and rolling them down her body. Her hands will sculpt her impression of beauty, and she will wink as a final gesture of approval.

My grandfather's hands were large and knobbly with long, slender fingers that billowed at the joints. His fingernails were slightly clubbed: convex and sloped as though they'd bowed under pressure or years of use. Although much slower as he aged, his hands were sprightly, lively—commanding in the way they cut through the air. I could remember them when they were sturdier, when they arched, sprang and contracted in flight, as though they were prancing or conducting an orchestra. Eventually they became more sedentary, carpal tunnel syndrome having dulled his fine motor skills. Delicate tasks like turning pages, or detailed work using his tools became near impossible.

My grandparents' hands connected and identified them in the world. You can often spot Deaf hands by the dexterity of the fingers: the fluidity and naturalness to the ways they can shift and bend into position. When I sign, my fingers are stiff and rigid. I cannot conjure the images that came easily to my grandparents. In sign language, voice and knowledge are embodied, much in the way a musician understands and relates to her instrument, divining the exact amount of air or pressure to apply to make it sing. The subtlest movements produce the shades of feeling only made possible through years of practice.

When Nanny signs, her signing space is small and held close to her chest, particularly when in public places. But in the privacy of her own lounge room or after a glass of wine, she blossoms outwards, always with a touch of melodrama in her long and liberal strokes. Her narratives unfold slowly, as though she's drip-feeding you details, sweeping you up in the arc of her arms and fingers, letting things linger and resonate in the wake of her movements. Grandpa was much punchier in his delivery. His hands were precise and emphatic, with pacing that dipped and dived, slowed and accelerated, and landed you with a bang where he wanted to leave you.

Like many children are soothed by the familiar tones of their parents' voices, there was something in my grandparents' hands that entranced and hushed me—something so distinctive in their respective styles that I'd find myself wishing for a way to capture it, store it for safekeeping.

When I was a child, I used to have a recurring dream about a family of ropes. There were no visuals in the dream, only tactile sensations in my palm where I held them all, knowing them each by their texture and the way they moved against my skin. I could sense when they were in conflict, when I needed to move my hands apart to prevent collisions and injury. I knew, too, when there was sadness, when the more frayed and delicate ropes needed me to cradle them gently. My hands were their home, and I shielded them from internal and external forces, and from those that might do them harm.

I was driven for many years by this image and by a protective impulse, especially when conflict arose in my family. I was often peace-keeping, especially between Mum and Nanny. Nanny was often a culprit of the 'deaf nod', a habit many deaf people can slip into when they're not comfortable asking for clarification. You can see it in her face as it happens, a dull blankness falling over her eyes. While Grandpa was at ease saying he'd missed something—perhaps because it happened so often—Nanny rarely let on.

'It's just pride!' Mum would cry when Nanny did it in conversations with her. She found it insulting. 'Doesn't she care about what I'm saying?'

I'd assure her she did, and that for Nanny it was about more than pride. It was about exhaustion and being burdensome. She didn't want to be a nuisance.

My father often struggled with my relationship with Nanny and Grandpa. In the last years I lived in the family home, he found it difficult to watch me disappear each morning to their house for breakfast. 'Running away to your other home?' he'd say as I met him in the kitchen on the way out the door.

He often bristled at our closeness, at the ways I gravitated towards them. I wasn't nearly so close with his parents. One night, while we were all having dinner next door at my grandparents' place, whatever had been irking him—the claustrophobia of living on top of one another, the strain of time spent with in-laws after a long day of work, my grandmother's post-war cooking habits—came tumbling out.

Nanny was busy ferrying food and utensils from the kitchen, laying them out before us, when Dad pulled a face and complained aloud. 'Christ!' he said, eyeing the unappealing slop of chicken casserole being dished onto plates. 'What the hell is this?' Dad often took advantage of having secondary conversations my grandparents weren't privy to. I couldn't hold my tongue. I told him he was being rude.

Nanny and Grandpa were watching, wondering what was being discussed. Neither Mum nor I had the heart to tell them. With our eyes we issued my father a warning and moved onto conversations about my university work. I was in the middle of a story about a day I'd spent at a school for deaf children, when my dad banged a fist to the table. 'I'm so sick of this deaf shit!' he spat, stopping me mid-sentence. 'Dad,' I said coolly, tersely, 'shut up.' He really lost his temper then, and said something about it being his house and how dare I speak to him that way. I reminded him we were at Nanny and Grandpa's, and perhaps he could learn some respect of his own. He left the room, leaving me in a silent fury.

I wasn't sure what set him off, nor that he could find the words to explain it himself. Dad was often generous with his in-laws. For most of his adult life, he had lived with them in some form. When Nanny and Grandpa came for tea at our place, Dad was particular about catering for them, cooking Grandpa's favourite meal of eggs, chips, baked beans and mushy peas.

Unable to sign and frequently forgetful about his face and body, Dad was probably the worst offender in leaving Nanny and Grandpa out. But as far as he was concerned, the four of us—Mum, Nanny, Grandpa and I—formed an exclusive unit that he remained outside of. Mostly, when we reminded him to accommodate them, he'd shift in their direction and repeat whatever story he'd just told. But sometimes he resented having to make the effort. In those moments, we argued with him, reminding him that a minor inconvenience on his part had a major impact on them.

On the night of the dinner, he accused me of hanging around my grandparents because I felt sorry for them. 'You always love the broken ones,' he said. 'The ones you can pity.' I don't remember what I said in response, only that it was a sharp and possibly unforgiving dressing-down. I went to bed furious that night, my hands clenched into fists.

•

My interest in hands is hardly surprising. They're central to Deaf iconography, and Deaf organisations use images of them in their logos and paraphernalia. Deaf memes and social media are bursting with hands, sometimes thrown in the air, clenched defiantly into fists, or held in the American sign for 'I love you'—the middle two fingers folded into the palm while the rest remain erect.

Much like other social movements such as feminism or Black Lives Matter, hands are political in Deaf circles. They are symbols of resistance and challenge to the status quo. This resistance can be seen in the enactment of Deaf applause, where hands are waved in the air, instead of clapped together. It's a small but significant act that champions the visual Deaf way.

The decision to use sign is also bold, especially given the ways it has been stifled throughout history. My grandparents' friends— plucky, determined people—were among those who took to the streets agitating for change and acknowledgement of their way of life, especially in relation to signing. In the 1980s they established lobby groups for various issues relating to Deaf people. I've inherited a folder full of old minutes and discussion papers from one such group. 'The Concerned Deaf' actively promoted Auslan as a community language in its own right. The papers belonged to a woman who was close to my grandmother. When she died, her hearing husband dropped many of her old things off at our house, and Nanny gave the folder to me. This small community initiative was instrumental in Auslan being recognised for the first time in the National Language Policy of 1987.

While manual languages may have been retrieved from the obscurity they suffered in 'the dark ages', they're no less free from longstanding ideas about intellect and ability. Though speech has always been privileged and deemed closer to thinking (and in some contexts, godliness), sign language disrupts the binary of brain and body through the synchronicity of thought and action. But the unmistakable physicality of sign means that old assumptions remain intact. Sign language is still seen as inferior, and its users are relegated to the status of second-class citizens.

The notion of class is a slippery, almost taboo, topic in conversations about deafness. Though deaf people are twice as likely to be unemployed than their hearing peers, are underemployed in terms of the range of occupations, and typically earn less than the general population in similar occupations, economic inequality is often the elephant in the room.

Australian advocacy groups like Deaf Australia cite communication issues, access to interpreters and the attitudes of colleagues and employers as significant barriers to deaf people in the workplace.

In a study undertaken in the UK in 2016, 56 per cent of deaf people said they had been discriminated against at work, and one in four had left a job as a result of discrimination. Despite significant changes to disability legislation and the creation of pathways to tertiary education in the last thirty years, deaf people in Australia have historically been hired in blue-collar positions. Even today, trades are one of the largest employers of deaf Australians.

Another study from the National Vocational Education and Training Research suggests that 'Deaf people are now better educated and some have broken through the barriers and are working in high-level positions; however, many are still streamed into a handful of potential employment areas that are seen as a "good" job for a deaf person.' While the younger generation move towards correcting this inequality, deaf people are subject to patterns of earning and living that reflect much about how hearing people think of them.

I never gave much thought to my grandparents' working lives. Like many working-class people of their generation, a job was a way to pay for the life they lived outside of its confines. Though they took pride in what they did, their careers felt secondary to the bigger, bolder things I loved about them. Where my mother and father strove towards middle-class prosperity, securing degrees and qualifications, climbing the property ladder and electing to live in 'the land of plenty', Nanny and Grandpa were creatures of a less frenetic time. They possessed the mild manners of those who knew their place. My grandparents understood that a ceiling existed between them and their aspirations. Being deaf precluded them from many occupations, and so they dreamed modestly. For the most part, they were content with their lot and accepted the limits of their position.

Nanny had a job cleaning houses for a few years in my early childhood, and I can faintly recall the final years of Grandpa's job at Airlite Windows in Windsor before he retired at sixty-five. I remember him shuffling off early in the morning and returning at dinnertime, when he'd play with us on the living room floor, still smelling of wood and metal shavings.

It was manual work he did there, stationed in the metal department of a big, open-plan factory, cutting window and door frames from plans he'd be handed on sheets of paper. Sometimes the jobs were standard, and other times they'd be custom made to satisfy the needs of the client. He would crosscheck the specifications, and then cut the aluminium to size with an electric pull-down saw.

When Grandpa arrived in Australia at the age of fifty-eight, my mother arranged an appointment for him with the Commonwealth Rehabilitation Service. It was a scheme that paid employers during a trial period as an incentive to encourage the employment of people with disabilities or deafness. Grandpa had to meet with a consultant for a comprehensive assessment of his skills.

In front of my mum, who came to assist with communication, and a young man who watched on with a clipboard and pen, Grandpa had to complete a practical assessment, demonstrating his prowess in various trades. He had to operate a drill and a lathe. Whenever he performed well, the man scribbled something on the paper, ticking things off his checklist. After a few weeks, my grandfather was assigned a place at Airlite, where he stayed for five years.

Like my grandfather, my grandmother worked all her life with her hands. When my mum and uncle were small, Nanny stayed home to care of them, taking charge of the domestic duties. The cooking, cleaning and organising were all her domain. But before then, she was a typist.

When Nanny left school at the age of eighteen, she studied at a typing college and earned a diploma. When she graduated, she could type sixty words a minute. She knew intuitively which letter belonged to which key. During her training she had to learn to type while blindfolded. With her eyes covered she had to complete the task by heart, her trainers observing to ensure she didn't cheat.

During lunch together one day, I asked Nanny about her working life, and she launched into story mode. She moved as though painting me a picture, her hands showing me the ways her fingers fluttered over the keys. Nanny's first and possibly favourite job was her role as a typist at the Cadbury Chocolate Factory in Bourneville, in the south of Birmingham.

At Cadbury, it was her responsibility to type up handwritten letters and business correspondence, taking care to correct spelling or grammatical errors whenever she came across them. She simulated the way she would pull completed documents from the platen, placing them in an imaginary tray at her side before making the sign for 'finish': two thumbs up and shaken from side to side before the chest. When the tray was full, she'd take them to one of the Cadbury brothers, who she insists were kind, respectable men who always thanked her for her efforts. One of them, she told me, had the most appalling handwriting and often joked about it with her. 'I'm surprised you can read it at all!' he'd say with a chuckle.

She stayed for six years and was promoted four times, a fact she delighted in announcing, making the sign for 'proud' as she did so: the backs of the fingers flicking the collarbone as though brushing dust from the shoulder. Laughing at her own boldness, she reached to the bookshelf to retrieve a Bible the Cadbury family gave her when she left to get married. 'They were devout Quakers,' she said as I ran my fingers over the leather cover and the gold lettering on the spine.

In the factory, she worked with many hearing people, but there were two other deaf women on staff, both typists like her. 'My colleagues at Cadbury were smart,' she said. 'There was one woman named Pat. She was completely deaf but could play the piano. Her parents taught her to keep in time with a . . . a . . .' Nanny's brow furrowed. She couldn't think of the word but rocked her index finger from side to side to show me what she meant.

'A metronome?' I suggested.

'Yes, that's it! She could read music and I was told she was very good. She took my job when I left. She was very skilled.'

Though most of her stories were upbeat, she recounted one experience with disdain. Sometime after my mother and uncle were born, my grandmother worked as a cook at the school my uncle attended. There she was under the instruction of a supervisor. 'Mrs Hickman was her name,' Nanny said, grimacing. 'She always looked at me and said, "Well, I never!" I always wondered exactly what she meant. She said it all the time, after everything I did!' Nanny shuddered.

'She was a nasty woman. Maybe she thought I was stupid because I was deaf. But I was always thorough with my work. Perhaps that's what she didn't like about me.' We laughed, and Nanny gave a dismissive flick of her wrists.

'What did you want to be when you were younger?' I asked.

'An air hostess,' she said. 'Or a library technician. I loved books, especially novels. But . . .' She pointed to her ears and shrugged her shoulders. 'I told your mum the other day that I think I would have enjoyed being a teacher. I would have liked to teach deaf children.' Nanny explained that in her time, deaf people were not permitted to teach in UK schools. In the same way deaf marriages were discouraged, so were deaf role models.

Words like 'discrimination' were rarely part of my grandmother's lexicon, but she reflected on how difficult things were for deaf people in the past. One of their closest deaf friends was forced to move to America in order to find work as a teacher. He taught in the United States for thirty years. 'Things are very different now,' she said, and disappeared into the kitchen to make a pot of tea.

•

For forty years, Grandpa worked as a metal pattern-maker in the Bean car foundry in Tipton. He'd received gifts for his years of service, which were displayed around the house. There was a gold watch for twenty-five years, and for forty, a cut-glass lamp that Nanny stressed was expensive, which sat on the sideboard in the living room, sparkling whenever the sun shone upon it.

One of the few work-related anecdotes I knew from childhood was one that Nanny used to tell. Grandpa had a skilled job, she always took care to announce, and had done well to ascend to the position of 'leading hand' where he was in charge of four other men. One day, the foreman of the foundry paid them a visit at their house. He sat down to tea with them, and while Grandpa was out of the room, told Nanny how impressed he was with his work, that he would have been promoted several times over if it weren't for his deafness. 'We'd need him to answer the phones,' the foreman explained. It was a requirement of all senior positions.

In 1948, when Grandpa was sixteen, he began there in the pattern shop as a carpenter. A distant family member had put in a good word for him with the boss. After a year, Grandpa wanted more of a challenge and moved to work with metal pattern-makers. In the early years of his career, he would help to make engine patterns onsite for the clients, but later on the companies would bring them ready-made, and the foundry men would cast them.

The Bean supplied the engines for Land Rover, Rolls Royce, Perkins and Austin. They cast the engines for the Mini car too. Grandpa never had anything to do with the assembly of the cars and tractors. It was only the metal components that the foundry used to produce, and Grandpa repaired and altered existing patterns with grinders and files. Back then, the Bean was one of several foundries across greater Birmingham that manufactured automotive parts, each of them responsible for different pieces of the final product. Headlights, seats, wheels and mechanics were put together by an array of people with different expertise. My grandfather understood his role as a small player in the game—a cog in the industrial machine.

I sat with him once, watching as he described the process of casting engine parts out of liquid iron, using a series of moulds and cores that set the shape of the items. When things got difficult to explain, Grandpa sourced a photo album and sat on the bed with me. He thumbed through images, his fingers getting stuck on the transparent protective casing. I pointed to things in the pictures and he gave me corresponding explanations.

Patterns, I learned, are a model for the object to be cast, a bit like a photo negative. Usually they'd be made from wood. A pattern would make an impression on the mould, after which liquid iron would be poured inside and solidify in the shape of the original design. The workmen would take the molten iron from the furnace using a ladle. The small ones could be held by hand, but the big ones were lifted by crane.

Sometimes, it was dangerous work. On the floor were iron plates and hulking great moulds that resembled giant sandwich presses when stacked together. One of Grandpa's colleagues died after becoming trapped in a mechanism during the night shift. The maintenance men found him the next morning, crushed in its jaws. 'They couldn't do anything for him. Gone,' Grandpa said.

My grandfather worked regular night shifts four days a week because the money was better. He'd eat dinner with the family and then work from six p.m. until six a.m. He'd return home on Friday mornings with his weekly pay packet and a small treat for his children: a bag of sweets each from the local corner store. As he collapsed into bed to sleep through the day, Nanny would sit in the kitchen and perform the weekly ritual of budgeting and organising their finances. Every Friday morning, like clockwork, she would take the brown envelope containing his wages in cash and divide it into piles: one for the mortgage, one for the car repayments, one for electricity, one for coal, one for groceries and one for Grandpa's cigarettes. By the end of Friday night, after the bills were paid, the money was gone. They never wasted it, but there was never anything left over.

Because of union action and frequent striking on behalf of the workers at the foundry, Grandpa often went several days or weeks at a time without income. He was never one to protest and kept his head down. But not wanting to upset his colleagues, he would strike in alignment with the union's wishes. To refuse to do so would result in being deemed a 'blackleg', a traitor to the cause, and an error of judgement that could ruin your reputation and see your membership suspended.

My mother thinks that many of the strikes tended to fall in the months leading up to Christmas. She can remember the threat of them hanging heavy over the family, producing anxiety, and the stockpiling of goods to tide them over. The fear of them was often worse than the reality. Still, a week without pay was enough to render things precarious.

The residue of those times lives on in my grandmother. Every year she buys her Christmas gifts up to six months in advance. When the presents have been bought, she lines them up on the bed in the spare room. For months they sit there, comfortingly tangible. Sometimes she checks on them as a hen would her brood, hovering at the doorway or gently touching each item in the spread, double- and triple-checking that nothing or no one has been forgotten.

•

My father's hands were always strong and competent. They fixed things and put bandages on wounds. But they were harsher than those of my grandparents. Even in gentler moments, when Dad might idly stoke my forehead or cheeks, the broken skin on his fingers, cracked and made coarse by chemicals in his garage, would scratch against mine.

Both Grandpa and my father had workshops where they spent hours tinkering on projects. Dad worked on his cars and bikes, and Grandpa had a knack for carpentry. There was furniture in their home that Grandpa had built when they lived in England: a mahogany coffee table with Queen Anne legs, a low-lying book-case in the same wood, a wooden train that was made for my uncle.

Their garages were full of tools and sharp objects, and for that reason, they were off-limits to us kids. On nights I couldn't sleep, I sometimes sneaked into my father's workshop to see what he was up to. Mostly, I was sent back to bed, but there were times he humoured me by explaining the difference between nuts and bolts, flathead and Phillips screwdrivers. Occasionally, I'd be given a menial task to do. I didn't care what it was. I did what I needed to stay near him.

But when we moved to our house with acreage, Dad built a shed down the back of the property, and by then I'd internalised rules about work for boys and work for girls. The shed was a distant place, closed off and impenetrable. For years, Grandpa's tools were kept in the garden shed, but as his carpal tunnel syndrome worsened, they were cast aside, meaning he focused more on his love of literature and cinema. I imagine my father might have watched my grandfather offer me his books and attention, and longed for the time I stood at the garage door, asking to be let in.

A grandparent's labour of love is far simpler than a parent's. Less loaded. I often observe the way my mother interacts with my nieces—the ease of their play and their unmistakable affection for one another. With my sister, Mum can be impatient. Without a common language, they butt heads much in the way I do with Dad. But with Zara and Imogen there's more room, an untempered generosity that manifests in small tokens—crocheted blankets for their dolls, puzzles and books, a trampoline for Christmas, a necklace Mum bought for Zara with the inscription 'I love you to the moon and back'.

My grandmother used to make us gifts. You could find her hunched over her white Janome sewing machine in her craft room, pulling fabric beneath the advancing needle, or cutting, assembling and stitching things together. She was always presenting us with new creations like table runners, patchwork quilts, teddy bears or handbags.

When my mother was a baby, Grandpa made her a rocking horse and painted it with a white face, black hooves, and a red mane and rocker. We still have it in the family home. Its eyes are fixed in a bashful expression, as though it is shy and peeping out from beneath its lashes. When I was born, my mum gave it to me, and then to my siblings. Today my nieces use it at my parents' place.

Back when I had it, the horse had two brown leather ears attached on either side of its head. But somehow, over the years, they've fallen off. 'Perhaps he's deaf now,' Grandpa joked a few years ago as he watched me playing with Zara, pressing the handlebars down so the horse jolted into motion. I laughed and said I liked the idea of that—a deaf horse made by a deaf man, to be handed down through the generations.

I had hoped that one day, should I be fortunate enough to have a child, that I might be able to lay them in the arms of my grandparents. I hoped they would cradle my little bundle and rock them back and forth like they did for me in my youth. Since time won't permit their meeting, I will bring that child to the deaf horse and sing them the song my mother sang to me, and which Grandpa sang to her. An anthem perhaps, of working-class tenacity: 'Horsey, Horsey, don't you stop, you just let your feet go clippity-clop. Your tail goes swish and the wheels go round. Giddy up! We're homeward-bound.'

I will tell them about their great-grandparents, the things they built and the stories they told, creating whole worlds between the movements of their hands.

14.

When I was little, my grandfather's ears were a site of wonder. I never paid my grandmother's ears much attention—hers are small and compact, tucked politely beneath her hair. But Grandpa's were large and prominent, announcing themselves to the world. They spanned the length between his brow and lips. I loved inspecting them, climbing onto his lap to see the droop of his pendulous lobes. I'd squeeze and tug at the elastic flesh, marvelling at the ways I could stretch it in all directions. Sometimes, I'd take the cartilage and fold it over, producing two flaps at the sides of his head. Grandpa would pull silly faces and I would laugh, and when he'd had enough of my probing, he'd take hold of my hands and pretend to gobble them up.

How could Grandpa's ears be so big and still not work? A couple of times, while seated on his lap, I gazed down the dark corridor of his ear canal. As I peered past protruding hairs, I expected to see a blockage. Maybe there'd be too much wax, and I could fetch an earbud from the bathroom. But I couldn't see anything. One afternoon, while Grandpa was watching TV, I pressed my mouth to his ear and yelled. He apprehended nothing, save the vibrations and the heat of my breath. I asked him if it hurt to be deaf. Did it throb like an earache? Grandpa laughed and assured me it didn't. I pressed him for answers, grappling to know how deafness felt. 'It just feels normal,' he said.

'Normalcy' means nothing to a child, and I had no sense, then, of the ways such a concept undergirded my grandparents' lives, the ways it functioned as a measure and benchmark of their success.

When I was slightly older, possibly seven or eight, my mother had an anatomical model of the human ear—the type you might find in a doctor's office—in her classroom at the school for deaf and blind children where she worked then as a teacher. The figurine sat on a shelf and was used to teach the science unit on 'The Senses' that was part of the grade one curriculum. The plastic pieces slotted together like a 3D jigsaw puzzle, and whenever I visited, I would sit on the floor, assembling and disassembling the parts.

Once, while observing me play, Mum told me the names of all the different bits. She pointed to the spiral coil of the cochlea, the curve of the auditory canal, and the fine bones of the middle ear. She showed me that the most important and sensitive parts were deep inside, and sometimes they didn't do what they were meant to. I nodded and turned the plastic pieces over in my hands, my gaze more forensic than before. I soon forgot the names she told me, but I continued to ponder that dark passage—the one that led from the world to my grandfather's head.

.

Deafness is considered a low-incidence disability, though one in six Australians are affected by hearing loss. On average, one Australian child is identified with deafness every day. One in every thousand babies is born with significant hearing loss, and by school age, this number rises to two in every thousand children. I used to rattle off these statistics countless times a day when I worked at a call centre for the Royal Institute for Deaf and Blind Children at the age of twenty. My job was to sell tickets for the Rainbow Lottery: a quarterly raffle-type competition with cash prizes. Money raised was given to educational programs funded by the charity.

The fundraising department was located on the same campus as the school my mother taught in, and sometimes we'd have lunch together and she'd listen to me complain about the difficulty of my task. With a script in front of me, and statistics at hand, I had to beg strangers to buy tickets to 'help the children'. Sometimes I got lucky, but more often I was told to fuck off or get a real job. Other times I'd be trapped on the phone while someone delivered a sermon about the state of Australian politics.

But there was something else in the job that sat at odds with me. To appeal to the hearts and minds of supporters, I knew I needed their sympathy. Against my instincts, I had to frame deafness in a way that suggested vulnerability and need. Daily, I reminded myself of the vital work taking place in the schools. I had seen it first-hand. From my desk at the call centre, I could often spy children playing outside in the preschool across the road. It was all for a good cause, I told myself. I knew the value and expense of proper support. But each time a kind old lady would purchase tickets for 'the poor dears', something would spear me in the gut.

A decade would pass before I found myself considering these statistics again, trying to make sense of deafness and the Deaf community that intersected with my world. I began looking at deafness from various angles. I treated it like a research problem: what did it mean to be d/Deaf? How was it a different way of being in the world? By asking myself what I knew, and what I didn't,

I found myself thinking of that anatomical model in my mother's old classroom. I had to concede that I had no medical or audiological knowledge, and I'd need to talk to those who did.

·

The university I work for is a short walk from the Australian Hearing Hub in North Ryde. In the years I was studying, I watched it being built, not far from the Arts building where most of my classes were held. One night, sometime in the first year of my PhD, I had a chance encounter with the hub's research program coordinator on a late-night bus to the city. When we struck up a conversation and I told her about my research, she invited me to tour the facility.

The first thing that struck me about the building was its size. When approached from the front, it resembles a giant container ship. Its twin towers are intersected by a stark white atrium, which ascends into the sky like a sail. The vessel's edges are sharp and angular—stainless steel trimmings, manicured lawn, orderly grass hedging—with swathes of gunmetal-glazed windows wrapped like sunglasses around its corners. Standing at the base of the five-storey complex, you'd swear it moves towards you, the pointed nose of the hull striding out to a bitumen sea.

The facility places researchers, scientists, educators, engineers and service providers under a single roof, with office space belonging to the foremost clinical practitioners in the field. There's office space for most of the country's notable hearing-related organisations and down the road is the global headquarters of Cochlear Limited, one of the biggest manufacturers of cochlear implants in the world.

Having spent my time on the other side of the proverbial fence, in the modest multipurpose rooms of the Deaf Society of NSW, I couldn't help marvelling at the slick, clean lines of the multi-million-dollar edifice. There were no overhead projectors or old PCs lying about here. The combination of money and clout made the Deaf Society seem dinky by comparison. It was no match for science, progress, technology.

Two research audiologists guided me through the various meeting rooms that day, through the labs and specially soundproofed booths where researchers and clinicians perform their tests. They brought me to the anechoic chamber; the room most photographed and featured in their promotional material. Located in the basement, beneath a complex design of concrete soundproofing and insulation, the chamber is custom built to eliminate echo. Inside, it looks like the set of a sci-fi film, or the interior of a spaceship. The walls and floor are lined with a grey foam-like cushioning that absorbs sound so that even the tiniest vibrations aren't felt. Researchers use this non-reflective room to conduct a range of controlled experiments.

After a few minutes in the space, I started to feel nauseated. Everything was deathly still. My footsteps and the sound of my voice were swallowed by every surface. My tour guides, who were entirely unfazed, told me that my response was common and related to my vestibular system—the system that gives us a sense of balance and spatial orientation, and is closely linked to the ear. In the absence of auditory feedback, my brain was scrambling to understand the lack of input. I was experiencing a kind of motion sickness, where the information from different sensory systems didn't match and made me feel ill.

In other testing booths, there were laminated graphs with headings like 'Adult grand mean waveforms', 'Inharmonic stimuli' and 'Development of cortical responses' thumbtacked to the walls. When my eye fell on a poster depicting a cross-section of the human ear, the pair took turns telling me about its three different parts: the outer, middle and inner sections. Pointing to the poster, they showed how sound waves travel from the outer ear, reflected by the pinna (the visible folds of cartilage on either side of our heads) into the ear canal until they hit the eardrum or tympanic membrane. 'The membrane is a very fine piece of tissue,' I was told, 'like a drum.'

Reaching for a piece of paper to demonstrate, one of the guides pressed his lips against its surface and began to talk. 'Put your fingers here,' he said. 'Can you feel the paper moving?' He explained then that with the right tension, the sound waves cause the membrane to vibrate at different frequencies, transmitting mechanical waves across three little bones, the malleus, incus and stapes, commonly referred to as the hammer, anvil and stirrup. These bones move and translate the vibrational energy through the oval window at the boundary of the middle and inner ear.

As the vibrations pass through fluid and hairs that line the cochlea—one of the most complex and delicate organs in the body— vibrational energy is turned into electrical impulses. Shaped like a conch shell or a snail, the cochlea comprises fluid-filled canals with differently charged ions. With the motion of the hair cells, channels begin to open, enabling the electrical energy to travel through the cochlear nerve and reach the brain. From air, to mechanics, to electrical energy—that's what the ear does. The process is called 'transduction'.

Reaching again for the diagram, he explained that transduction can fail in many parts, but the two major sites of failure occur either in the middle or inner ear. In the middle ear, people can suffer 'conductive loss' where bones become ossified, or infection occurs. It is more serious when the inner ear is affected, referred to as 'sensorineural loss'. This is the type associated with illness, genetic loss or age. 'Your grandfather's deafness would have been sensorineural,' he offered. I had mentioned Grandpa's meningitis earlier in the day. 'His illness would have permanently damaged his inner ear.'

As I drove home that day, listening to the radio, I imagined a wall of sound approaching my ears. I pictured the invisible waves as though they were beams of coloured light, rippling against membranes and bones, making their way to my brain.

In the months after that initial tour, I became a frequent visitor to the hub. I developed friendships with staff and relished the occasions I bumped into someone by the elevators, or in the monochrome cafe downstairs. I welcomed the exchange of ideas and papers, the generous and collaborative research culture I encountered.

The first time I socialised with the audiologists was at a make-shift bar on the university campus. We drank sangria outside on the wooden deck and listened to a string of performers hired for a one-off festival. When an electric guitar wailed from the nearby stage, and a grungy-looking rock band trudged into view, the audiologists dived for their handbags and trouser pockets. Noise-cancelling earplugs were retrieved and crammed into their intended sockets, while mine were left unadorned and at the mercy of the music.

In between acts, we swapped stories about our projects. I told them about my interest in Deaf culture and history, and many of the team shared anecdotes about their clinical practice and experience. One man told how fulfilling he finds it to work with cochlear implant recipients. He told me about an eighty-nine-year-old man from Perth, who flies all the way to Sydney to work with the team at the hub. 'Being able to help people like him is really the highlight for me,' he said. Others echoed this sentiment and stressed how they wanted to make a difference to people's lives.

Like so many healthcare professionals, the best audiologists wanted to help. I found this admirable, but as with other conversations about 'vulnerable populations', the question of how to help was up for debate.

That evening, we talked through sensitive issues such as cochlear implants (CIs), informed choice and the ethics of implanting children. We discussed the importance of bilingualism and access to sign language. Words were chosen carefully and diplomatically by all.

At certain junctures, we disagreed, sometimes strongly. At one point, someone crinkled their nose and shook their head: 'I'm sorry, I just don't understand some Deaf people,' they said. 'The world is hearing! If they're eligible, kids should get an implant.' Another jumped in to quell the fire: 'It's about culture, though,' they retorted. 'Try to imagine that your way of life was under threat.'

From the outset, I was aware of the likelihood that I would think in drastically different ways from my audiologist peers. Deaf friends and colleagues from the school where I was volunteering had warned me about 'AV Nazis'—a term they use to describe supporters of auditory–verbal methods of therapy where deaf children learn to listen and speak using their residual hearing. Permanent use of hearing aids and cochlear implants are encouraged under this method.

The sign for this particular type of enthusiast are the letters 'a' and 'v', followed by an index finger placed under the nose like a moustache. On a weekly basis I had seen audiologists visit the school. Some of them would give signed instructions to children, but I understood this to be a rarity. Before I visited the hub, I had assumed I'd be walking into a giant AV camp. For a time, I was splitting my days between two opposing poles of the deaf-related world. At the school and at the Deaf Society, I kept the fact of my fraternisation with medical folk to myself and felt at times like a traitor who had crossed into enemy territory.

Many people assume that cochlear implants are a medical miracle, championed and celebrated by the community they're intended for. It's a great surprise to hearing people to learn of their controversial history over the last forty years. Since the 1980s, Deaf people have reacted with hostility to the development of this technology, and have mobilised to protest their use, particularly in young children who cannot consent to the surgical procedure, which involves an internal component being screwed into the skull. An external part adheres to the head with a detachable magnet. Where a hearing aid amplifies sounds, an implant bypasses most of the ear by putting out electrical signals to the brain.

Cochlear implants have been seen as an attack on Deaf culture. Some have likened the medical intervention to cultural genocide— a weapon of normalisation that limits a child's capacity to access signed language because of the emphasis placed on speaking and listening with the device. Even today, decades after the supposed end of oralism, many leading deaf-related organisations discourage the use of sign in CI recipients.

Part of the issue is rooted in questions of identity. The very implication that deafness needs to be cured infuriates Deaf people. Some Deaf parents even hope for deaf children in order to pass along their cultural and experiential heritage. In 2008, a British Deaf couple sought to use IVF to select a deaf child from a mix of deaf and hearing embryos. In response, parliament passed the *Human Fertilisation and Embryology Act 2008*, to prevent selecting embryos with a 'serious physical or mental disability'. This case sparked outrage and was seen as a bioethical conundrum. Many thought the couple were unhinged and cruel to wish deafness upon a child. But in this case, desiring a child in one's own image was less about vanity and more about unity. To inherit deafness is to inherit a language, a culture, a community.

Since the 1980s, much has changed in discussions of CIs. Though there are still people who staunchly oppose them, I know of proud culturally Deaf parents who have given their children cochlear implants and raise them to be bilingual. There are many Deaf adults who, in their twenties, elect to undergo the surgery, and see the device as a tool that can sit alongside their Deaf pride. Identity politics shift and grow, just as the technology does. Nevertheless, cochlear implant companies are giants, and their power can't be underestimated. In 2019, before the pandemic hit, Cochlear Limited's annual profit was $276.7 million.

Cochlear implants are an Australian invention. The modern multichannel model was developed and commercialised by Grahame Clark, who in 1978 surgically implanted a prototype in a forty-eight-year-old patient. In 1985, after a series of clinical trials, the US Food and Drug Administration approved the use of the implants in adults, and six years later, in infants as young as six months old. Since then, over 330,000 registered devices have been implanted worldwide.

Australia has one of the highest implantation rates in the world. In the United States, an estimated 59 per cent of profoundly deaf babies receive CIs, and 51 per cent in the severe range. In Australia, the number is as high as 98 per cent for candidates below the age of two. It's worth considering, too, that 90 per cent of deaf children are born to hearing parents, most of whom are steamrollered by shock and uncertainty about how to proceed. And, because of the prevalence of universal newborn auditory screening, parents are directed only to medical advice at the time of their child's initial diagnosis.

This isn't the case in other parts of the world. In the UK, for example, a national program is in place to help people make informed choices. Professor Wendy McCracken, who specialises in the education of the deaf at Manchester University, helped design this program. When I met with her in West Yorkshire, she explained their approach. 'We try to explain that if you give a cochlear implant, these are the implications of it. Likewise, if you go sign bilingual where you focus on sign language, these are the implications. We try to give them all the options.'

She suggested that the rate of implantation is much higher in Australia because of 'very strong drivers saying "this is the way forward".'

Parents of deaf children are placed in the precarious and seemingly impossible position of choosing what is right for their child. The barrage of information they receive is often confounding and conflicted. Most audiologists will advocate for early intervention, meaning children are fitted with hearing aids from birth, or with cochlear implants from just a few months old. In a baby with radio aids, new moulds would need to be fitted every ten days. With cochlear implantation, there is a window that must be observed in order to maximise the efficacy of the technology. When a child's brain is young and plastic, it is best placed to develop language through listening. This time-sensitivity means that many parents leap at the opportunity to help their children, believing an implant to be the panacea for their 'ills'.

Though there is no empirical evidence to support it, hearing-related organisations (and their clinicians) suffer from a longstanding belief that sign language harms the acquisition of spoken language. Evidence of the superiority of cochlear-implant and spoken-language-only approaches is also poor, with much research emerging around the benefits of access to sign. Researcher Wyatte C. Hall even claims, 'Cochlear implants are unreliable standalone first-language intervention for deaf children.' Because implants require years of training in order to be useful, many deaf children spend the first years of their lives in a state of language deprivation. An implant does not mean a child becomes hearing overnight. Learning to hear, through hours upon hours of audiological training, is an intrinsic part of the cochlear implant experience.

Research shows that deaf children of deaf adults outperform their peers with hearing parents on several fronts. Deaf of Deaf, as they're colloquially known, are at an advantage, given they are signed to from birth, and thus the language centres of their brains are stimulated without delay. Even in homes with no spoken language, these children are more likely to learn fluent English than deaf children of hearing parents who use English at home and go to a mainstream school. As Andrew Solomon writes in *Far from the Tree*, 'Deaf of Deaf also score higher in other academic areas such as arithmetic, and are ahead in areas like maturity, responsibility, independence, sociability and willingness to interact with strangers.' Deaf people will often cite the Deaf of Deaf phenomenon as evidence that undermines the grand narrative of scientific and technological progress.

Despite the advent of infant screening and improvements in technology, deaf and hard-of-hearing children continue to experience a range of issues relating to literacy, cognitive, social and emotional development. The ongoing polarised conflict about which systems families should choose for their children—either sign/bilingual or CI and speech—ends up standing in the way of real developmental needs. 'Just give them *language*,' Deaf people urge from the sidelines. Many argue that withholding a perfectly viable intervention such as signing constitutes a medical harm. Researchers Matthew Hall, Wyatte C. Hall and Naomi Caselli sum it up well when they write, 'Language deprivation is a phenomenon so rare among hearing children that it is seldom seen outside famous cases of severe developmental pathology or criminal abuse/neglect, and yet so common among Deaf and Hard of Hearing children and adults that it often fails to provoke the alarm it deserves.'

Another sticking point relates to the fact that cochlear implants are permanent devices. It's not a surgery that's easily reversible. You can't just change your mind down the track, for example, and put a hearing aid on top of an implanted ear. Though the risks of infection and complication are low, during the surgery the ear, nose and throat surgeon makes a cut in the cochlea in order to connect it to the device. This means the device may destroy residual hearing that can never be restored. Though techniques are rapidly improving, some people lose all their residual hearing. On top of this, many people aren't candidates for implantation. In cases where deafness is caused by injury or absence of the auditory nerve fibres, a cochlear implant cannot help.

There are also misconceptions about the quality of sound a deaf person can access through a CI. If you listen to simulations of speech and other noises heard through the device, there is a distinct discrepancy between sounds produced with the aid of the technology and sounds that a hearing person can access. Although it's impossible to fully replicate, computer-generated approximations sound synthetic and robotic, like Donald Duck played through a distortion pedal or synthesiser. This does change over time—the more the brain hears, the more it processes. Nevertheless, the training required to truly hear is laborious and time-consuming.

Cochlear implants consist of a mic, a processor and a receiver with an electrode array. The electrodes and receiver are inserted into the cochlea, which acts like a hair cell replacement and stimulates the cochlea directly. Hearing people have thousands of hairs that allow them to process a range of sounds, while cochlear implants have only about two dozen channels that correspond with audible frequencies. Despite constant improvements, they are designed to pick up speech sounds, but are less adept at relaying the complexity of real-world sounds, particularly in regard to pitch and timbre. Their function in noisy environments is also temperamental at the best of times. In many public places, CI recipients are no more able to hear despite the fact of their implant. This is also true of occasions where batteries die, or during bath or shower time when the external component cannot be worn. In these moments, you remain functionally deaf, and without sign language, arguably limited in your ability to communicate.

Because of the labour involved in listening, some cochlear implant users like to schedule 'cochlear-free time' where they temporarily detach the external magnetic component. Many of my Deaf friends with implants will take these breaks for the sake of their mental health and say that detaching the device can feel a bit like taking your bra or shoes off after a long day.

My grandparents had discussed cochlear implants with me in the past. Grandpa was uncertain about them. 'I don't know how I feel about it. I don't like it really,' he'd said. 'I've been deaf almost all my life. I should be used to it by now.' When a couple of their Deaf friends elected to have implants in their early eighties, Grandpa was critical. 'Yeah, they can hear sounds,' he said, 'but they've no idea what they are, or what they mean. They take those things off and they're still deaf as a post.' I asked him if he'd ever contemplated one for himself. He looked a little dumbfounded. 'I suppose,' he said. 'But it would be too "in-between". You'd hear only some noises, and then lipread the rest. I'd rather have proper hearing or stay as I am.'

Nanny felt differently. 'I'd have one in a heartbeat if I could,' she said. She told me that if they'd been available in her youth, she was sure her parents would have scheduled the surgery, no question. 'They would have wanted me to have every opportunity, every means for success.' Now that she's in her late eighties, she wouldn't want the hassle of an operation, nor the comprehensive auditory training that would be required for her brain to process the new stimuli.

During my visits to the Hearing Hub, I volunteered myself as a test subject in some of the research projects underway. I subjected myself to audiometric screening, EEG and eye tracking experiments, where the effort of listening is measured by electrodes attached at various points on the head.

Before the main experiment, I needed to undergo a routine hearing check, performed by one of the research assistants. Earphones were placed in my ears and a series of beeps were played to assess the threshold of my hearing across a range of frequencies. Each time I heard something, I pressed a little button, and the information was then logged in an audiogram produced by the research assistant, who handed me a small slip of paper with my results marked on a graph. 'Everything is in the healthy range,' she said, and smiled, before showing me how I'd scored, little black crosses to indicate activity in my left ear, and circles for my right. 'Your hearing is normal.'

Disability Studies scholar and CODA Lennard J. Davis writes about the pervasiveness of 'normalcy' in western cultures. He reminds us that normalcy is a relatively recent idea. Up until the late nineteenth century, there was no such word to describe the concept, at least none that reflect its current manifestation. The word 'normal' only enters the English language around 1840. Likewise, the word 'norm' in the modern sense has only been in use since around 1855. Davis observes an ideological shift around this time, citing nineteenth-century preoccupations with statistics, eugenics, Darwinism and the emergence of the bell curve as key factors that erect 'the hegemony of normalcy'. Such hegemony has functioned since, he says, to maintain the perception of deafness and disability as a deficit.

When my grandparents were young, audiology didn't exist. It was then a nascent, developing science. Audiometers were invented in the mid-1920s, but the term 'audiology' wasn't used until 1946, six years after Grandpa had gone deaf, and twelve after Nanny. In the same year, the first degree in audiology was offered at Northwestern University in the United States. In Australia, as in other parts of the world, audiology emerged as a field shortly after the Second World War, largely in response to deafened soldiers requiring rehabilitation. In 1947, the National Acoustic Laboratories were established, and within a few years had centres operating in most major cities in the country. The first Australian audiologists were trained in such centres, eventually leading to the development of the Audiological Society of Australia in 1968 and establishing the field as it is today.

Neither Nanny nor Grandpa can remember being tested with audiometers, but Grandpa can recall appointments with a specialist where a tuning fork was used to measure the extent of his deafness. The doctor held the metal apparatus, striking it to make it ring, and moved it above Grandpa's head, asking him to report when or if he heard the sounds produced. My grandfather heard nothing. When he recounted the experience, he shook his head and said what a useless, insulting encounter it was. He wanted the doctor to leave him be.

I didn't really understand the cause of his irritation until I sat in the cushioned armchair of that testing booth myself. Though every audiologist I worked with was pleasant and took care to ensure my comfort, I felt like a lab rat. As they poked and prodded me with various implements, and scraped my scalp with a syringe filled with conductive fluid to ensure a good reading with the electrodes, I wondered if this was akin in some way to what my grandfather felt as his doctors fussed about him with a tuning fork. But I am hearing, and my place in these experiments was to produce the baseline data. My results would be used as an example of standard function. They would be measured against those deemed as abnormal. I did not, at any point, have to carry the knowledge that my grandpa did: that in the eyes of his doctor, he had, or perhaps was, a problem to be fixed.

15.

Nanny has always liked to tell me the story of my first visit to England. I've watched her perform it several times, her body narrating alongside her voice. If I close my eyes, I can see it: my grandmother before me, shoulders rounded, cooing and cradling an imagined infant in the crook of her arm.

The story began at Heathrow Airport. Nanny and Grandpa had come to collect my mum and me after the twenty-four-hour flight from Sydney. I was three months old. 'I was waiting and waiting,' Nanny would say. She'd show me how she craned her head to see over the crowds in the arrivals lounge. Then, her erect index finger would be used to represent my mum emerging from the terminal. It bobbed up and down across the space before my grandma's body.

'I ran!' she'd say, thrusting her balled fists back and forth as though sprinting. 'I ignored your mum and got you.' She'd use the sign for 'ignore', and then reach beyond her body to grab at the air. Her hands would scoop towards her chest, and she'd dip her head to nuzzle the cheek of the bundle in her arms. Gazing at the bundle's face, she'd make a long, tender, yawn-like sound that rumbled in the back of her throat: 'Awwwhhhhh.'

'I was so excited—my first grandchild! You stayed with us for five weeks. I couldn't put you down.'

When it was time to fly back to Australia, my mother's friend came to Nanny and Grandpa's to take us to the airport. Grandpa was working a night shift, and Nanny was left home alone. Five minutes after we'd gone, the doorbell flashed. It was Mum, coming back to check on Nanny. She was still crying in the hall.

•

My grandparents loved to speak of England. They made it no secret that they were British first, Australian second. When they watched international sporting matches, they cheered for their homeland unless they'd been knocked out of the competition. Nanny courted an affection for all things English: the heft of nostalgia finding expression on the walls of their home. They followed all news of the Royal Family, and images of Great Britain and the Black Country were framed and hung among pictures of us kids. When I once mentioned the idea of Australia becoming a republic, my grandparents were horrified to learn that I supported such a notion.

My grandfather was particularly proud of his Black Country heritage and had explained how the area of the Midlands got its name from the various coal mines, iron factories, brickworks and steel mills that left a covering of soot over the land during the Industrial Revolution. The pride was so pronounced that for his eighty-fourth birthday we threw him a 'Black Country'–themed party with print-outs of beloved landmarks pinned up among the streamers and balloons. He was devout in his love for his football team—the Wolverhampton Wanderers—just as he was in staying up to date with the news from the *Express and Star*. Sometimes he'd tell us old jokes, most that hinged on the regional accent and idioms. 'The Black Country alphabet' was often cited, but sounded like gibberish to us: 'A is for opple, H is for 'oss, O is for Ow-am-ya?'

When I was little, it was Nanny and Grandpa's Britishness that stood out more to me than their deafness—the English foodstuff in the cupboards, the HP sauce, mushy peas and packets of Angel Delight. The way they pronounced the words 'yoghurt' and 'garage' differently from my Australian peers and family. My mother, who was much more of a chameleon, retained a soft accent, but always pronounced things the Australian way. Nanny and Grandpa were sticklers, creatures of pride and custom. I suppose, too, they couldn't hear the difference in sounds, so never adopted them.

After months of nagging, Nanny began to keep a jar of Vegemite in the house for when the grandkids came round. It was strange to me that she stored it the fridge. We always put ours in the pantry. Sitting atop her kitchen bench with my little legs dangling over the cupboards, I'd watch her blot it sparingly onto pieces of buttered Wonder White. She'd pull faces of disgust in my direction, her mouth shrivelling as though she'd sucked a lemon.

As I grew, I became curious about the places my grandmother would rhapsodise about. I pictured rolling hills, woodlands and gardens, hedgerows and oak trees, elms, birches and willows, cottages covered in honeysuckle, and bluebells in fields of green. My head was full of images wrought by Enid Blyton in books like *The Faraway Tree* and the Famous Five series. At bedtime, I often read these with Nanny and stepped into the kinds of imagery that has long captured the Anglo-Australian imagination. In later years, I grew wary of this expatriate romance and all it obscured about the colonial history of our nation. But back then, England seemed an enchanted place.

My siblings couldn't have cared less about Nanny's stories, and often rolled their eyes at them. It was hard to stomach her sentimentality, and sometimes the musings felt barbed, almost accusatory. My grandmother made it clear that we were all missing out on beauty, history, culture, all of Europe at one's doorstep. In reaction, perhaps, my sister doubled down on her Australianness. When my parents took us to the UK when I was sixteen, they brought us to all the tourist landmarks and the family ones too: the old homes in Coseley and Sedgley, Denise Drive, Shenley Avenue, and Dingleview. While I watched on with wonder, Lizzie complained that everything was old and ugly.

In more recent years, when I'd sit on their living room floor, recording on my phone, Nanny would speak of her teachers and the sweeping grounds of her high school in Newbury. With legato phrasing she'd describe the gardens and the manor house where she boarded with three other girls in her dorm.

Grandpa spoke less, preferring to show maps and dig out artefacts I might find interesting. One time he spread a map of Greater Birmingham across the table between us and traced the route from Dudley Zoo to his childhood home in Wallbrook. As a five-year-old he'd walked the two-mile journey after becoming separated from his parents on a family outing. I watched him outline the route he took. He knew all the street names by heart, speaking them aloud as the paper crackled beneath his moving finger.

I once asked Nanny and Grandpa what it was like to move here so late in life. They looked at one another before Nanny spoke. 'To live in Australia was different for us. It wasn't easy.' There's a tone of voice my grandmother reserves for talk of England. Her register changes, like a car shifting gears, becoming wistful and dense with breath. Little puffs of air punctuate her sentences whenever she tells me how they packed their life into cardboard boxes and shipped it all by freight. For years after arriving, Nanny had terrible heat rash and felt faint even in the winter. Her best Marks and Spencer overcoats were exiled to a dusty corner of her wardrobe.

Since emigrating in 1990, Nanny and Grandpa travelled to England twice, once in 1995 and again in 1999. In the years in between, they wrote letters home. Nobody had a TTY, so this was their single mode of contact. Nanny remembers the first trip home was during the British summer. Both of her parents were living in a nursing home. The last time she saw them she left in tears. Her mother's arthritic body was doubled over in a wheelchair. She was so badly bent that Nanny had to crouch on the floor to read her lips. Her father had also recently suffered a stroke. On the day they visited, he couldn't remember who Grandpa was.

I can still remember the day that my great-grandfather died. I'd just finished my first year of school. My mum had to break the news to her mother. She drove us three kids, all under the age of five, to Nanny and Grandpa's. When we arrived, Mum told us to sit quietly on the couch. My grandmother was collapsed into a green armchair, looking pale and drawn. Mum stood above her and rubbed Nanny's back as she heaved into her hands. I can still recall the raw, guttural sound of the sobs.

'Didn't you ever want to go back home again after the second visit?' I asked them one afternoon. 'Oh yes!' Grandpa exclaimed. 'But money, and then health . . .' He pointed to his own body, rapping his knuckles against his chest. 'Life got away,' he continued. 'And the family came out to visit, too.' My great-auntie Beryl came for his sixtieth, and my great-uncle Lawson and auntie Mavis came twice. He rattled off a list of friends who had also made the journey.

As part of my PhD, I travelled to England to conduct research. My thesis was focused on d/Deaf people's appreciation and perceptions of music—the ways it functioned in their everyday lives. I wanted to understand its cultural significance and the terrain it occupied in the Deaf community. To do so, I had scheduled interviews with Deaf musicians and was due to work with 'Music and the Deaf', a UK-based charitable organisation that provides workshops, performance opportunities and support for deaf musicians of all ages. It is arguably the only one of its kind. Knowing I'd be there for some weeks, I also planned visits to Longwill (previously Moseley Road) and Mary Hare School for the Deaf, Nanny's alma maters.

When I told my grandparents I'd been in touch with current staff members and would be staying onsite at Mary Hare, Nanny squealed and jumped up and down. She squeezed me till I gasped for breath. 'I can't believe it,' she said. 'You're going to my school!'

My grandmother reached for my hand and pulled me into promenade position. Together we waltzed around the room. 'Oh, I do wish I could come with you,' she said, clasping her hands together. Grandpa sighed. 'You'll have a fabulous time, though.'

I was due to arrive in the British spring and Nanny assured me the weather would be glorious. I might only need a cardigan for the evenings.

On the morning I departed Sydney, I had breakfast at Nanny and Grandpa's. They were excited for me, but there was a heaviness in the room too. They said it was just because they'd miss me. I'd be gone for over a month, after all. But as I turned to leave, Grandpa sighed, and recited a line of poetry: 'Oh to be in England, now that April's there.'

I cocked my head to the side, and made the sign for 'what?'

'Look it up after,' he said, and kissed me goodbye.

16.

'Oh, to be in England
Now that April's there
And whoever wakes in England
Sees, some morning, unaware,
That the lowest boughs and the brushwood sheaf
Round the elm-tree bole are in tiny leaf,
While the chaffinch sings on the orchard bough
In England—now!'

—*Robert Browning*

I arrived in the UK on an unseasonably cold April morning. After landing at Heathrow, I searched the high street shops for a winter coat, scoffing at my grandmother's rose-tinted predictions about the weather. On the train from London Paddington, the sprawl of apartment blocks turned gradually into fields of yellow rapeseed and when the signs for Newbury approached, I felt strangely giddy. As my taxi entered Mary Hare School for the Deaf, and the sprawling grounds came into view, I had to catch my breath. There was no exaggeration. It was as beautiful as Nanny had said.

The school sits on multiple hectares of land, about fifteen minutes from the centre of town, with Snelsmore Common Country Park just across the road. The main building, named 'Arlington Manor', or 'Manor House' in my grandmother's time, is a stone Georgian manor with a climbing rose up its front and wisteria vines stretched across the main archway. Once owned by aristocrats and used as a residence, its stately facade looks as if it belongs in a period drama. Hedgerows lead to the main entrance, and the gardens are replete with spherical topiary and a water feature. A conservatory looks out to expanses of green.

The setting was at once foreign and familiar to my Australian sensibilities. It was the kind of place I had seen in television shows and adverts about the motherland. It was nothing like the schools I'd visited in Australia, certainly not the deaf schools, which were cheerful but small, often underfunded and closing at rapid rates.

Though far from extravagant, the inside of Arlington Manor is impressive. The ceilings are ornate and high, and a grandfather clock sits on the far wall of the reception area, chiming on the hour. The building has the air, or perhaps the illusion, of permanence— 130 years of history captured in portraits of past head teachers on the walls. A thickset mahogany staircase leads to the second storey of the manor, where the school principal at the time of my visit, Peter Gale, had his office. In a disused fireplace, a television sat under a mantelpiece in the foyer. On the days I was there, it played footage of students at various work placements and school events.

The first time I met Peter, he descended from the top of that sweeping staircase. As he approached, interview footage of him happened to flash across the TV. 'Who's that horrible man on the screen?' he said, and laughed. When we sat down together, Peter wanted to know the nature of Nanny's memories. He seemed wary of interrogation, ready to defend his turf should it be required. When I said they were happy, he exhaled. 'You find with past students from your grandma's era,' he said, 'that they either have stories about their time at school being the best years of their life, or they're really angry.'

'Oralism really was something different back then,' he mused. 'You hear horror stories, and you can't imagine what it was like.'

For the duration of my stay, Peter gave me the use of 'West Lodge', a quaint yellow-brick cottage with Georgian bay windows. Used to house guests or to temporarily accommodate the families of students who come from across the country, the lodge sits on the perimeter of the school grounds, surrounded by a forest of pines. I slept in a room with lemon-coloured walls and linen, and each morning, wandered past the rhododendrons towering over the driveway to have breakfast with the students in the refectory. Later, I sat in on their classes, had meetings with staff, and explored the grounds.

On that first day, I video-called Nanny and Grandpa. Nanny leaped off her chair when she saw me. I flipped the camera around so the pair could take in the scenery. 'My school!' she crooned, clasping her hands together. She looked as though she might dive through the screen. I took them past the garden and the tennis courts. 'Same!' Nanny said and signed at once, 'It's just the same as before!'

Out of school hours, I watched impromptu football matches and was introduced to the care staff that supervise the children in the evenings and over the weekends. Just as it was in Nanny's time, students board through the week and return to family on a Friday afternoon. But for some, home is too far away, meaning that they need to stay onsite for the entirety of the term. I joined the remaining students for trips into town. I sat with them on the coaches owned by the school and caught wind of discussions about the upcoming prom. On these excursions, I watched the older students go off independently into shops around Newbury village. Some of the sixth-formers had casual jobs in the ticket hall and snack bar of the Arlington Arts Centre—a performance hall open to the public and located on campus, which hosts a number of arts, comedy, music and drama productions each year.

Because I was used to much smaller schools in Sydney where my mother had worked, the sheer scale of everything at Mary Hare came as a shock. The deaf school where I had volunteered for a time had only thirty pupils across primary and secondary combined. Mary Hare had over two hundred enrolled in secondary alone.

Mary Hare is the biggest deaf school in the UK and is renowned for its high standard of education both nationally and overseas. In Deaf circles, it's a distinguished institution. Named after its founder—a suffragette and humanitarian who established the original site in 1916 in Burgess Hill, Sussex—the school relocated to Newbury in 1950. Princess Margaret officially opened it in that year, arriving on the estate in a helicopter. Nanny was present that day. She boarded between 1948 and 1952 and remembers curtseying before the princess. She stood at the edge of a red carpet with girl Guides on one side and Boy Scouts on the other. There were pictures of it all through the newspapers at the time.

Back in my grandmother's day, when it was a selective grammar school, students needed to sit an academic test to enrol. The school no longer has this requirement but remains high-performing. It is one of the few deaf schools that stick to the national curriculum. I was struck by the confidence of many students, some who approached me to chat. I was warmed by the close relationships of peer groups I observed in the common rooms of an evening as they played music or games together. But what really stunned me was the presence of British Sign Language outside of the classroom. My grandmother couldn't have imagined such a thing. The school's policy was so strict back then that she didn't see signing until she first went to a Deaf club.

As I sat in the dinner hall at mealtimes, I found myself gawping at the flurry of hands engaged in conversation. The excitement I felt, the warm flush of recognition and familiarity, was often tempered by my outsider status. I felt like a voyeur as I tried to work out the meanings of BSL signs. There were bits I managed to grasp, and figuring out signs through context gave me a little rush. But still, it served as a reminder: I was an interloper.

I had felt that way too at the schools for deaf and blind children my mother worked in over the years. At North Rocks, I knew the layout of the buildings—the Renwick College library, the brightly coloured monorail in the playground at Alice Betteridge School— like they were part of my own backyard. The campus was a kind of stomping ground, and I spent many sick or pupil-free days alongside my mother in the classroom when she couldn't find anyone to look after me. I would sit with my books, peeking out to catch glimpses of my mother tending to the kids. She was in her element. But even under Mum's wing, I was never quite in mine.

Once, Mum came to my school and taught my class some braille and the handshapes of the Auslan alphabet. As she held the floor and the attention of my peers, I sat there swelling with pride. When she was gone, a certain weight was also lifted. The natural way of things was restored—Mum was at her school, and I was at mine. Though deaf and disability education felt like it ran in my blood, it belonged more to my mother than it ever did to me.

•

Here at Mary Hare, staff used spoken English to communicate, and conversations among students took place in all sorts of ways. Many signed silently to one another, some spoke and signed simultaneously, and others were decidedly verbal. There was a seamlessness to the ways they changed their linguistic hats depending on their company. They were able to flit between communication styles to match their peers' preferences.

Peter had explained to me that the school modernised its old policies on communication. He told me all students are either severely or profoundly deaf and use speech and English exclusively in class. During break times, or in the TV or dining rooms, they're free to use what they wish. 'You know,' he said, 'we were previously telling them off all the time. And it never felt quite right in the late twentieth century to be stopping people using a communication mode that they've grown up with, or they'd had at their previous schools.' Later in the week, I spoke with another teacher about the use of sign at Mary Hare. 'Oh yes,' she said. 'We don't have a "sitting-on-hands" policy anymore.'

When Peter spoke of the school and its philosophy, he lamented the double bind of 'inclusion' and the misconceptions about what this means for deaf populations. In the last thirty years, schools for the deaf have suffered a similar fate to Deaf clubs. In the UK, the Consortium for Research into Deaf Education found in 2019 that ten dedicated teaching units for deaf children were closing each year. The trend is similar all over the world. More and more, children are sent to 'regular' mainstream schools so that they can be socialised in the hearing world. Though well-intentioned, this practice can often lead to deaf children feeling isolated and dependent on inadequate itinerant support.

Though terms like 'special needs' are frowned upon in current disability discourse, there is something to be said for specialised education. There's a painful irony in the fact that 'inclusiveness' in mainstream schools can result in exclusion both socially and educationally. Deaf kids can feel singled out for their difference or otherwise miss out on crucial information. As many deaf children face linguistic barriers, the pace and style of address in a hearing classroom can mean that they fall behind. Research shows higher educational outcomes for deaf children who have access to visual language, and the social, emotional and academic benefits of deaf schools are undeniable. Yet as parents are steered towards mainstreamed education, deaf schools are seeing budget cuts and lowered enrolment numbers.

As Peter explained, 'A criticism of a school like ours is that we segregate the pupils—keep them in a bubble, and when they leave, they'll flounder because the outside world will be too hard for them.' He shook his head, fatigued by the flaws of such logic. 'We say no. If you build their self-esteem, their literacy, their actual qualifications, they can hold their heads up high and learn to self-advocate. And that's our evidence, and that's who, in the main, our young people are.'

The benefits of this approach were obvious to me. Mary Hare's class size was small, with eight to ten students in each secondary class, and four to eight students in primary. Classrooms were acoustically treated to ensure the best listening environment and a high staff-to-student ratio made sure that no student was left behind. All teachers on staff were specialised Teachers of the Deaf who are trained to understand and provide for the unique learning requirements of deaf children.

When I spoke with the heads of audiology and speech and language therapy, they explained the value of children having constant onsite access to their services. When batteries failed or technology malfunctioned, they could see and treat issues as they arose, rather than having to send the child home or to an appointment off campus. In the hour I stood talking to members of the audiology office, three pupils dropped in to have their devices adjusted before class.

Within school hours, many of the students received speech therapy, and I sat in on their sessions. In each appointment the therapist provided the students with different targeted activities, tailored to their stage of development. The first session was with a girl in fourth form. The therapist tested the girl's hearing aids, producing a hoop-like filter instrument behind which she made different sounds, and asked the student to repeat them: 'sss', 'shhh', 'esss', 'eeee'. The next student, whose native language was Latvian sign, worked on irregular plurals. He was given flashcards and had to read them aloud: pyjamas, fish, binoculars, trousers and tweezers. He didn't know the last word but performed the action of someone plucking an eyebrow. Another boy, whose home language was BSL, was distracted by my presence and asked me questions about Australia. When I responded and he didn't hear, I glanced at the therapist, who nodded and allowed me to sign my answer.

In the classrooms, all of which were set up in horseshoe configuration, pupils were connected to Mary Hare's group aid system with an interface that connects to their cochlear implants or hearing aids. The unique system was developed to optimise listening in classroom settings. The teachers ensured that pupils were connected and could follow along with the lesson. Everywhere I went, there was a palpable 'deaf-can-do' attitude. Students were preparing for work experience at local businesses—many of them were placed at the national headquarters of Vodafone, which Newbury (locally known as Voda-ville) is famous for. As I walked through the halls, I noticed pictures of alumni were framed with a blurb below about their chosen careers. Among them were paediatric nurses, graduate engineers and TV production managers. At the top of each photograph was the text: 'Set your sights high!'

The optimistic ethos was palpable. There was no denying the array of opportunities the school had on offer. It even had a burgeoning music department. Peter explained there were clear pathways to university, as well as a vocational program that encouraged community ties and engagement. Students were encouraged to choose whichever path best suited them. But I couldn't help but feel uncomfortable about a lack of choice when it came to language. While there was a relief in seeing sign creep onto the premises, the language policy in the classroom constituted an indelible kind of gatekeeping.

The school my mother taught in was a sign bilingual school. There were Deaf teachers and teacher's aides on staff—cultural and linguistic role models who taught in sign as well as English. At Mary Hare no such modelling could occur, at least not for BSL users. There was nothing to stop Deaf teachers working at the school— prohibitive policies had long moved on from my grandmother's time—but they'd be required to teach in English, which could alienate Deaf applicants. There were four deaf teachers and teaching assistants, and eight deaf support staff at the time I visited. I was also pleased to learn that the school had a wellbeing coordinator who was qualified in BSL, and I saw interpreters coming and going on campus, but I wondered about Deaf mentorship and the value of language role models.

Faced with the success of Mary Hare's academic results, I wondered if my thinking was too utopian. English, Peter would maintain, enables choice, gives access to the wider world. The ongoing belief in the supremacy of English seemed phonocentric, paternalistic even. Maybe my idealism amounted to naivety, but I wanted something more radical than tolerance of sign language. More diverse than bolstering the dominant tongue.

I wanted the school to continue its role as a bastion of Deaf education. I wanted teachers of the deaf to continue their specialised training and safeguard the futures of these young people. But did it depend on speech in order to do so? Was there no more room to wind back the oralism of the school's history?

I was confronted directly by this history one afternoon, as I rifled through the school archives, opening boxes of old records. Inside them were newspaper cuttings and photographs, academic transcripts and programs from awards ceremonies. I found my grandmother's name in a program for the Annual Speech Day from 1951. She won the prize for speech that year and was listed as a prefect and the lacrosse vice captain. I saw the names of some of my grandparents' friends and there were photos of the headmasters Nanny had mentioned in stories—Mr Mundin and Mr Askew— who were in charge in her time. When I spotted Nanny in several photographs, the admin women in the office exclaimed at my luck and gathered round to see.

As I read her list of achievements in the transcripts, I felt a twinge of guilt. I'd tended to be dismissive on occasions she spoke of them. I remember once, after a conversation took place with a home-care nurse who came to shower Grandpa twice a week, Nanny was insistent on explaining something to me. I'd been sitting on the back deck, when Nanny and the nurse came outside to join me. They were having trouble understanding one another and Nanny asked me to interpret. Eventually the conversation turned to what I was doing. Nanny told him that I was writing a book. He smiled and nodded. 'She must get it from you,' he replied. 'Well,' said Nanny, swelling slightly, 'I did go to a grammar school. I passed all my exams and did very well!'

As the nurse turned to go back inside, I smiled and shook my head. Nanny spoke to me sternly then. 'It might look like I'm showing off, but I'm not,' she said. 'I'm fighting for Deaf people. I want to show hearing people what we're capable of.'

On the final day of my visit, I was taken to see the girls' dormitories in the old manor house. Based off Nanny's descriptions, I managed to find the room where she had slept over sixty years ago. I stood in its centre taking in the shock of makeup on the dressers and posters of heartthrobs and idols stuck over beds. My grandmother's bed was the one closest to the window and I pressed myself to the glass, looking out at the tops of trees and the vast stretch of green lawn across the grounds she would have once admired.

That afternoon, the school's head of audiology took me to a little village called Chieveley where Nanny used to cycle to church every Sunday. As we drove, she attempted to recreate the route Nanny would have taken, winding me through all the back streets and pointing out the new motorways that have popped up in more recent years. I wandered through the church and the graveyard adjacent, feeling as if Nanny was somehow beside me.

My grandmother was always superstitious and interested in otherworldly or inexplicable things. She used to speak of guardians who watched over her and was entranced by shows that had a spiritual bent. *Highway to Heaven, Medium* and *Crossing Over* were among her favourites. She collected anything with angels on it, and in the gardens at home there were statues of angels in the flowerbeds, angel-covered candleholders and figurines in every room. She had other tales about people leaving signs for her after they'd passed. One of them featured a picture frame that repeatedly turned itself upside down. My mother called this a bunch of nonsense, but it didn't deter my grandmother. She went on weaving her tales about the mysteries of the universe.

Though I didn't share my grandmother's beliefs, I couldn't help but see signs of her wherever I went. I did double-takes of old ladies in the cobblestone streets of town, and everything seemed to take on a charmed quality. Each morning in Newbury, I woke to the sound of foreign birdcalls. I turned down the bedclothes and looked outside at blackbirds and robins in the trees and bushes that lined the private road leading to West Lodge. On strolls through the grounds and in Snelsmore Common, I saw rabbits, deer and pheasant, and laughed at the absurdity of feeling caught in a children's picture book. And then, one day, it snowed. I ran outside, watching it fall, feeling as if I were witnessing a kind of magic.

As I drew the curtains each night, I thought of my grandmother and her stories. I imagined her drawing her own curtains at home, a sight I've seen a million times. Geographically, my grandparents had never been farther away. But here, in her school, in her country, I felt Nanny's presence like a ghost, lingering in the strange crispness of the English air.

17.

For much of his life, Grandpa retained his memories of sound. Some were wispier than others, but many remained imprinted on his mind. Among them was the memory of whistles blown through the fingers, the glottal bark of sea lions he once saw at the Dudley Zoo, and his mother's raised voice whenever she would reprimand him. She used to call him a 'varmint', delivering the word with an upward inflection.

He remembered evenings spent around the family wireless, his older brother, Alan, sitting right beside the speaker. He could recall the signature tune to his mother's favourite BBC radio program, and once repeated it for me in a singsong voice: 'It's Monday night at eight o'clock, oh can't you hear the chimes. They're telling you to take an easy chair, to settle by the fireside, take out your *Radio Times*. It's telling you that Monday night at eight is on the air.'

But the most vivid of these memories—the ones that seemed to intrigue and haunt him—were those of echoes.

At the end of his street in Wallbrook, where he lived as a child, there was a grassy hill that overlooked the neighbouring village. He and other local boys used to play there, and affectionately named it the 'rock-a-bank'. They used to scramble to its peak and yell over the fields and rooftops. 'Coo-ee!' they'd cry, cupping their mouths, and waited to hear their voices resounding through the valley. As they roamed through the streets of Wallbrook, Tipton and Coseley, they bellowed into tunnels and against the underside of bridges that overhung the canals. Everything reverberated. It was as though the sound had a life and will of its own, rearing itself again and again as it passed through the hollow space.

By the time he was nine, Grandpa had moved to Birmingham to attend his new boarding school. On weekends during his early teen years, when he was permitted to leave the school grounds, he spent hours meandering through the canals off Broad Street. Birmingham was affectionately known then as 'The Venice of the Midlands', and my grandfather came to love its network of waterways and boats.

But never again did he shout into tunnels at the water's edge, chasing the whelp of his voice as it ricocheted from surface to surface. He was deaf and absorbed this new place with his eyes. Echoes, like other auditory phenomena, would become remnants of his past.

•

After leaving Newbury, I travelled to Birmingham to stay with my great-aunt and uncle, Mavis and Lawson. Grandpa's brother and his wife had hosted me in years gone by and had visited Australia a few times in my youth. I felt at ease in their home, perhaps because it reminded me of Nanny and Grandpa's.

Their house was full of familiar knick-knacks. There was Wedgwood china on the shelves which looked just like Nanny's, and on the mantelpiece were figurines of women in bonnets and floating white dresses. One of my grandmother's patchwork table runners was laid across the dining table, and in the sunroom were paintings of Sydney Harbour they'd collected during their travels.

Spending time with them was like experiencing my grandparents by proxy. Lawson sometimes felt a strange facsimile of my grandfather. He was a few years younger and slightly thinner, but there was a strong family resemblance—the same long face and wide grin.

Though I had a busy research schedule, Mavis and Lawson volunteered to chaperone me everywhere, driving me round in their zippy red hatchback. In between my appointments with musicians and educators, they took me to old family haunts: the church where my parents were married before they came to Australia, and family homes. We drove past the pub that Grandpa used to frequent, and the old Bean foundry, both of which had closed and had new businesses emerge in their places.

In the evening, my great-uncle fetched old photographs of the three brothers, Alan, Melvyn and Lawson, and spread them over the coffee table. From a trinket box he retrieved old love letters and postcards sent between my great-grandmother Lily and great-grandfather Edgar during Edgar's deployment with the navy in the 1920s. As we looked through the contents, we spoke about Lawson's childhood memories.

Lawson would have been four when Grandpa was hospitalised with meningitis. He doesn't remember much about their life before then, only that their home in Wallbrook was struck by lightning on the day of his third birthday. The family were asleep inside and were lucky to escape unharmed. The side of the house and the entire staircase was blown to pieces. Lawson remembers they had to jump down from the second floor to flee the wreckage.

"It was in the papers and all,' he told me. Accompanying the article was a photo of Grandpa and Alan playing in the garden while emergency services assessed the damage. For a time, the whole family moved in with the boys' grandparents until they found a new home in Coseley.

I asked Lawson what it was like to grow up with a deaf brother and heard echoes of my grandfather in his response. 'It was quite ordinary for me,' he said. 'It wasn't an obstacle.' Lawson told me how Grandpa devised a system for communicating after dark when they were boys. The pair shared a room when Grandpa was home from boarding school. Once the lights were out, they used their hands to 'talk'. Holding onto one another, Grandpa would ask questions, and Lawson would listen to his older brother's instructions: 'Squeeze once for "yes" or twice for "no".' If the questions were more open-ended, the sequences were more elaborate: 'If you want X, squeeze three times,' 'If you want Y, squeeze four.'

While Grandpa was away at school, Lawson once found a book on ASL and surprised his brother by learning to fingerspell. Only he'd unwittingly learned the American one-handed alphabet, not knowing there was a difference. Though they never really signed to one another beyond this, Grandpa was impressed. Eventually, he learned the English vowels and consonants. 'I was quite blinkin' young,' he said, 'but you don't forget these things.'

Lawson remembers the family travelling on the bus into Birmingham to the deaf school when they'd go to visit Grandpa. It was war time, the early 1940s, and in those years Birmingham was often bombed during German airstrikes. To get to him, they'd drive past rubble and burned-out buildings. His mother insisted they go. It was difficult to be apart, especially because she'd never wanted to send him away. It was only when her brother sat her down and convinced her that she agreed to it. 'You must let him go,' he'd told her. 'It'll be the best thing for him.'

•

For months, I had planned a visit to the site of my grandfather's old school in Edgbaston. It was marked in my mind and in my calendar as an important expedition. I knew it had closed down in the mid-1980s, but that some of the buildings remained. Grandpa had told me the headmaster's house was still there and the wood-work classrooms too. They had been repurposed and turned into office space by the charity that moved into the premises in 1984.

Though it wouldn't be the same as the visit I took to Nanny's school, I had imagined it as a kind of pilgrimage. I thought I might walk the perimeter of the property and catch sight of the old sporting fields at the back, where Grandpa had played cricket and football. I was determined to take photos of the premises and bring them back to Australia.

With my great-aunt and uncle in tow, I walked from the centre of town to the outskirts of Edgbaston. The night before, Lawson sat with a tattered street directory and planned our route, staying up late to study the map. When we arrived the next morning at Birmingham New Street station, I was led past the new city library, passing cranes and workers as they shifted pylons and poured concrete. Everywhere we looked there were construction and demo-lition sites. The sound of jackhammers wailed around us.

We walked in single file, Lawson striding out in front, mumbling to himself as we reached familiar checkpoints. When we came to an underpass in the city's southwest, we lost our bearings. Though we'd been walking for well over an hour, the school had managed to evade us. After a while, we approached the corner of the street we'd been searching for, but struggled to find signage or markings to indicate the different lots. When we came to a worksite that stretched down the block, I asked a workman in a hardhat and hi-vis jacket for directions. 'Number four?' he said. 'You're here!' He pointed behind him, and my stomach lurched.

What was left of the buildings was covered in scaffolding. The yellow arm of a crane loomed above, and a barbed-wire fence stood between us and him. Hanging from it were signs that read 'Keep out' and 'No access for unauthorised personnel'.

Grandpa's school was being demolished.

It seemed fitting to me, somehow, that my grandfather's history was disappearing before me. Though Nanny's past seemed to fall in my lap, I had to dig and chase for Grandpa's, unearthing it in tiny, often intangible bits. Where my grandmother is an open book, Grandpa was a labyrinth, replete with complex twists and turns— pathways barricaded off or leading to tunnels with locked doors at their ends. Sometimes he would lower the gate and let me rove through the rooms of his mind, many of which were brilliant and grand. But others would remain closed and off limits, at which points I'd have to be limber, my prying eyes sourcing alternate in-roads.

I was struggling to write about my grandfather, too. Having tried over the years, I could not pin him to the page. At every turn I was defeated. A file I'd dedicated to Grandpa in the 'notes' program on my iPhone somehow got corrupted, meaning I lost valu- able late-night insights and snippets I'd gathered. On my first day in Birmingham, I found out that the Wolverhampton Deaf Club in Rupert Street had closed down only a month or two before I arrived. I heard later that it had reopened elsewhere, but at the time it felt as if a trail had gone dead.

Standing in front of the barbed wire that day, I must have looked as crushed as I felt, because the man in the hi-vis offered to help me. When I told him I'd come all the way from Australia, he led me to a demountable office where a woman explained the plan to redevelop the site into retirement villas. She said that many of the buildings would be torn down, but some were being restored. Before I turned to leave, I remembered that Grandpa had mentioned a blue commemorative plaque that used to hang at the main entrance. I asked about it, and she told me she'd get her team to have a look around for me. 'It might take a while,' she warned, so we sat outside and waited.

·

The only photo I had of Grandpa's school was taken from the fields at the back, so I had no sense of its facade from the street. Grandpa had described the main building; 'It was similar to an old stately home,' he had said. The boys slept upstairs in large dormitories with up to thirty of them in the room. The girls had their own separate quarters on the other side of the building.

When they enrolled, children were given a number that was used when issuing clothing, textbooks and other supplies. Grandpa was number 51. It was printed above his bed. The teachers often called the children by their numbers, and many deaf people of my grandparents' generation had these numbers as sign names. When Grandpa told me this, I grimaced and said how dehumanising it seemed. Grandpa shrugged it off. 'That's just how it was,' he said.

Though we'd had multiple conversations about it, I couldn't quite make sense of the school's educational philosophy. I knew from my own research that it had begun as an oral institution, and Grandpa had said that his teachers instructed him in English. Photos from around 1900, held by Birmingham Archives and Heritage, show the use of both oral and manual methods being used. Other accounts suggest a decline in the use of sign language in the first half of the twentieth century.

In a book called *Out of Sight: The experience of disability* by Stephen Humphries and Pamela Gordon, there's an entry from an ex-pupil, who attended the school in the 1920s. The woman shared that they were never allowed to sign in class and were often smacked on the hands, or had their arms bound for whole mornings or afternoons. She recalled one occasion where her teacher caught her signing to a friend under the desk. The teacher was angry and told her she looked like 'a little monkey'.

Our conversations about school were often stymied. Even on good days, questions I thought to be simple produced complex or roundabout answers. It was clear that certain lines of inquiry were uncomfortable, especially when I probed about oralism. I asked my grandfather if his teachers ever signed to him, and he looked at me as though I were mad. 'Of course not,' he snapped. 'But they did make up rubbish signs sometimes.'

'Like gestures?'

Grandpa nodded.

'So you weren't supposed to sign?'

'No, not in class.'

Grandpa told me he'd never been punished for signing. Mostly, the teachers looked the other way if signs snuck into class. But there was one teacher who wouldn't permit it, especially when out in public. Sometimes groups of children were taken for sojourns into Birmingham city, walking in crocodile formation to the botanical gardens or the cricket grounds. While they were out and about, the school and its pupils were 'on show', and Grandpa intuited that signing on these occasions was improper.

Like Nanny, Grandpa spoke warmly of his teachers: Mr Wallbank, Mr Jones, Mr Nixon and Mr Dickens. Mr Dickens had taught him in physical education and woodwork, and Mr Jones was the man responsible for kindling his love of literature. Grandpa could remember reading *Treasure Island* in class, and Mr Jones gave him his own copy so he could read ahead of the others without hindrance.

He told me about Mr Wallbank, whose wife baked Grandpa a cake on his twelfth birthday. His sign name reflected the moustache that snaked across his upper lip: an index finger traced beneath the nose. Wallbank arrived at Edgbaston during the war years when many of the other teachers were sent away to fulfil their national duty. By the end of the war, Mr Nixon had returned after serving in the air force. He was Grandpa's last teacher.

As an adult, my grandfather had opportunities to meet with these men. When he was about twenty, he ran into Mr Nixon out in the Deaf world. Upon spotting him in a crowd of young deaf men, Nixon pointed to Grandpa and exclaimed, 'Ah! The clever boy!' It was a memory Grandpa liked to recount. Mr Wallbank remembered him too, even forty years after he'd left school. Grandpa got in touch with him, knowing he'd relocated to Derby. Upon visiting a friend in the area, Grandpa asked the man's hearing daughter to call him on a number they'd sourced from the phone book.

When he answered, and the young woman explained she was speaking on behalf of Melvyn Hunt, Mr Wallbank was cheery. 'Oh yes!' he said. 'The boy born on February the twenty-ninth.' He invited Nanny and Grandpa to visit his house, and then later to a restaurant for lunch.

For years I had wondered where my grandfather developed his apprehensiveness about sign language. I'd tried to map the small wounds from conversations with my mother, or the culture clashes that stacked up over the years. But I had the sense that I was missing something. I'd often seen Grandpa become small in public, attempting to shirk the scrutiny of others. I particularly noticed it when we went to cafes together and I'd begin signing unabashedly at the table. He'd become unresponsive, putting a hand over his good eye as though cradling his head. During arguments, he'd retreat to that same position.

I also knew that Grandpa had shied away from giving a speech at my parents' wedding. It wasn't customary then to use interpreters, but even as it became the norm, Grandpa never used them. He came around to the idea in the final months of his life when it was difficult for Mum to interpret while remaining fully present in making end-of-life decisions. But at the wedding, in a room full of hearing people, Grandpa wasn't comfortable signing or speaking. He asked Lawson to read on his behalf. It was hard, particularly for my mother, to understand this alongside his Deaf pride.

One afternoon a few months before my trip, as we sat watching *Great British Railways*, a missing fragment of insight clicked into place. The episode had been filmed near his school and Grandpa began to speak of the children in the manual class. 'The manual class?' I asked, shocked. 'I thought your school was oral?'

'Oh yes,' he said. 'We used both. But the manual class was for the special kids.' He paused then, trying to be diplomatic. 'The ones who couldn't learn the hearing ways. You didn't want to be in that class. We knew what it meant.'

I wanted to wail. But there was nobody to hold to account. In the months after that conversation, I cultivated a hunger for Edgbaston. I wanted to bear witness to that place—to stand where Grandpa had stood and stare it down.

Perhaps there is no reckoning with a faceless structure, something my grandfather had long come to accept. As historian Nicolas Mirzoeff writes: 'Oralism was not simply evil or ignorant, but was able to command both governmental and intellectual support.' It was powerful because whole structures of thought held it up. On occasions when I'd huffed about injustices in the name of oralism, Grandpa had looked at me, almost with sympathy. 'They thought they were helping,' he said.

•

I waited with Lawson and Mavis outside the site manager's office on a bench for a few hours before a worker emerged with a dusty blue item in his hand. When I saw him approach, I sprang from my post. Brushing dirt from its surface, he laid the plaque in my hands. 'Nearby the site of The Old Royal School for Deaf Children', it read. 'Established 1812. Closed down 1984.'

I ran my fingers over the text. Mavis stood beside me and kept thanking the heavens. Lawson laughed and shook his head. 'Blimey,' he cawed, and rubbed my shoulders.

The manager let us stay with the plaque for as long as we wanted, and we took turns holding it, passing it round like a sacred object. As I handed it back, I asked the workers if they'd re-hang it when the job was finished. They assured me they would. I returned it to their care, taking a final moment to squeeze it to my chest.

That afternoon as we wandered around by the canals, I thought about something I'd read by Iain Sinclair. A building is a reservoir of memory, he writes, and cities are like palimpsests, written upon over and over, containing within them the residue and resonances of time gone by. Birmingham was laden with such residue, and the sediment of my grandpa's past was being stirred up and written over in my presence. His was a disappearing history and a swallowed kind of sadness. I knew it was a matter of time before I'd be left with only resonances of him—trace elements of a life gone by.

Spying a bridge up ahead with no one in the immediate vicinity, I hurried beneath it, taking a moment to myself. At the water's edge I had the urge to scream. Instead, I hummed three notes, and listened as they rang out, echoing in the underpass until they disappeared.

18.

There's a popular saying in the Deaf community: 'Deaf can do anything except hear.' My grandmother recites it to me often. But if deaf people cannot hear, can they participate in or understand music? I had wondered about this for many years and decided it was a question answered best by Deaf musicians.

I left Birmingham station, waving goodbye to Mavis and Lawson at the platform to travel north to Halifax, West Yorkshire. As part of my research, I'd planned to spend a fortnight in the company of charitable organisation Music and the Deaf. I'd be shadowing Danny Lane, a Deaf pianist and head of the charity, following him along to the various music workshops, public lectures, group rehearsals and signing choir practices run by members of his staff.

I had met Danny the previous year when he came to Australia to work with deaf children at a local Sydney school. He'd given a stirring presentation about the ways d/Deaf people were able to access music, sharing his own experience as a sign language–using, culturally Deaf musician.

Years after I'd hidden my love of music from my grandparents' sight, I became curious about the ways d/Deaf people experience it. I discovered that my grandparents learned to play musical instruments at school. They had lessons about percussion and rhythm. Nanny had played the triangle and Grandpa the drums. In assemblies they sang hymns and recited 'Bless this house'. 'Sang or perhaps said them,' Grandpa had quipped. 'I don't know how good we sounded.'

Stuffed in a drawer in my grandfather's desk was a manila folder full of sheet music. Over the years he had collected print-outs of his favourite songs and stored them there for future reference. I hadn't known of the file's existence until, some months into my research, Grandpa went in search of it one afternoon during one of our many chats on the back deck.

When he handed it to me, I flicked through the yellowed papers. I found sheet music for 'I've Got Sixpence', 'It's a Long Way to Tipperary' and 'Danny Boy'. 'I like the Irish songs somehow,' he said.

The contents of the folder shouldn't have been surprising. All of Grandpa's favourite films were musicals. As a kid, I used to sit with him and watch 'Oliver', 'Yankee Doodle Dandy', and 'Singing in the Rain'. He liked 'Mary Poppins' and 'The Sound of Music' and tried (and failed) on many occasions to win me over with 'Bedknobs and Broomsticks'.

Every year, Grandpa watched the Edinburgh Military Tattoo and the BBC Proms. He loved marching bands, and especially enjoyed the different formations, the choreography and how the instruments moved when played. He liked the trombones and the drums best for the ways they showed him the music, the ways the tubular slide jerked back and forth, and the flurry of drumsticks rapping against the snare. 'I like the movements,' he told me. 'I can't hear it, but I enjoy it just the same.'

Nanny was also taken with music. Every week on a Sunday, she sat down to an episode of *Songs of Praise*, a BBC program where church choirs perform Christian songs in picturesque parts of the country. More recently, I've caught her watching episodes of *The Voice*. When I asked her what she liked about these shows, she spoke of the beauty of singing faces. 'They look magical,' she said. 'Almost like angels.'

Music might seem, at first, an odd area of focus when it comes to the Deaf community. In the minds of most, music and deafness are strange, incongruous partners, and the term 'deaf musician' is a curious oxymoron. But the involvement of the deaf with sound and music is far from strange.

Deaf people have a long history with music. The best-known example is Beethoven's deafness during the latter part of his career, where he was said to have cut the legs from his piano so he could immerse himself in the vibrations as he played and composed. Other reports suggest that he used a wooden stick or pencil held between the teeth and the piano in order to feel the sounds.

Today, there are several Deaf and hard-of-hearing musicians who work and teach in music-related fields, most notably the Scottish percussionist Evelyn Glennie, who describes her body as a resonating chamber. Glennie is a classically trained pitched percussionist who began to lose her hearing when she was eight and was profoundly deaf by the age of twelve. She studied at the Royal College of Music in London, and throughout the decades of her career has earned an OBE and DBE, along with fifteen honorary doctorates from universities in the UK.

In her TED Talk, 'How to Truly Listen', Glennie explains how her deafness led her to understand and practise 'listening' in a new way. She claims that her job 'is all about listening. And my aim, really, is to teach the world to listen.' But far from focusing on the ears, she shows how music can be perceived by opening up the entire body. When Glennie learned about pitch with her teacher, she would place her hands on the wall of the music room in order to connect with the sounds. She learned to feel the vibrations of notes created by her instruments. The low notes she feels in her legs and feet, and the high sounds in various places on her face, neck and chest. 'Hearing,' she reminds us, 'is a specialised form of touch.'

There are Deaf raves that have run for nearly twenty years in Europe. At these inclusive events, the bass is pumped through multiple loudspeakers, there are light shows, vibrating dancefloors, sign language interpreters, induction loops and performances from Deaf dancers and DJs. Signed song is increasingly popular. Most bilingual schools for the deaf run signing choirs, which often promote and become associated with cultural and linguistic pride. And in mainstream performances, sign language interpreters are appearing next to artists to render music more accessible to d/Deaf audiences.

Deaf rap and hip-hop are also popular. In 2009, Finnish rap artist Signmark became the first deaf person to get a recording deal with an international music label. Deaf American hip-hop artist Sean Forbes also became popular after getting a two-record deal with Eminem's producer in 2010. Both artists perform using their native sign language and have a large Deaf following. In Australia, Alter Boy are a group of three Deaf musicians who combine electro pop with Auslan in their performances.

But music has long been a fraught subject in the Deaf world, even a taboo. For many Deaf people, music is considered a hearing pursuit. It can be understood as part of the 'Audist establishment', which imposes hearing norms and interests upon the d/Deaf.

Because a common-sense understanding of music relies on its capacity to be heard, it can be seen as a form of normalisation or cultural colonisation.

For this reason, some deaf people reject music and find no place for it in their lives. When I visited one of my grandparents' deaf friends in the UK, she told me that music and deafness together was 'nonsense', almost offensive. The suggestion that d/Deaf people might enjoy it was anathema to her. Some Deaf people are indifferent about it. 'Music? What for?' they say. 'I'm Deaf.' Others have a keen interest in music and advocate for its place in the Deaf world.

Deaf DJ Troi Lee has spoken publicly about the need to acknowledge deaf people's involvement with music. 'We need to reverse the myth that deaf people can't enjoy music,' he says. 'I want to show the world that deaf people can play music just as well as our hearing peers.' But the role of music in deaf lives is so contentious and polarising, that in 2017, Deaf singer Mandy Harvey, who made it through to the finals of *America's Got Talent*, was sent death threats from within the Deaf community. The backlash against Harvey condemned her for promoting 'a hearing activity'. Such is the predicament of the deaf musician. They often have to prove their worth to the hearing world and their loyalty to the Deaf community.

My grandfather didn't care about the politics. He went on collecting lyrics and sheet music, tucking them away in his folder. He liked words and he liked them set to music. One year, when the Military Tattoo toured Australia, my mum booked tickets for her and Grandpa to attend. Grandpa asked to be seated as close to the speakers as possible. He wanted to feel everything.

•

The headquarters of Music and the Deaf were housed in a heritage-listed building beside the Halifax train station. On the day that I arrived, Danny showed me around the space—a small, shared office with a couple of desks, a kitchenette, a music room littered with instruments, a piano and filing cabinets full of teaching resources.

At the time of my visit, the group's founder, Paul Whittaker, had recently retired after twenty-seven years of work. When he established the group in 1988, Paul wanted to bring music and deaf people together, providing services, support and opportunities for deaf people in the arts. Over the years, Music and the Deaf has produced many musical projects like the Deaf Youth Orchestra that toured the UK in 2012, and 4ORTE, an ensemble of four professional Deaf musicians—pianist Danny Lane, trumpeter Sean Chandler, flautist Ruth Montgomery and violinist and vocalist Eloise Garland. All the musicians in the 4ORTE group are music graduates, with some completing their training in esteemed conservatoires.

My schedule for those weeks was bursting with appointments. I went with Danny to community events in Bradford where deaf students experimented with instruments and technology in after-school sessions. I had meetings scheduled with members of 4ORTE. I visited schools for the deaf to see their weekly signing choir practices. One of the groups was working on the song 'Jai-Ho' from *Slumdog Millionaire*. Their conductor explained to me that she normally teaches them her interpretation first, explaining the song's meaning as she goes along. From there, the kids tend to take over, offering up suggestions, adding or refining signs. 'It's a process of negotiation,' she said.

As I watched them practise, one boy raised a hand and suggested a change to the sign for 'cry'. Rather than sign it in the usual way, he suggested two fists raised to the eyes and rotated at the wrists.

The conductor put the change to the group, who voted to accept it. The students ran the song the whole way through, throwing themselves into the performance. Their signs were emphatic and precise. In a break between run-throughs, a girl from the junior school told the group she'd been watching Bollywood dances on YouTube and asked if they could incorporate a dance move into the piece. She came out the front to demonstrate it. The conductor asked the others what they thought. 'Yes? No?' she signed. Fists were thrown in the air in the handshape for 'yes'.

When I met with trumpet player Sean Chandler, he told me about his kinaesthetic relationship with music. He explained how he takes his shoes off when he plays so he can feel through the floor. When performing jazz, he also stands close to the drummer in order to stay in time. 'Sometimes I play with one of my feet on the side of the drum,' he said. 'Especially if the crowd are being noisy. There have been times where I've sat on the bass drum, too.'

Sean found it curious that most people think music is some-thing you just hear. 'You know when you remember something, and you sing it to yourself?' he asked. 'I kind of feel it here,' he said, pointing to his throat. 'When I play the trumpet, a lot of it is muscle memory.' He took out his hearing aids then and placed them on the table before us. 'Ready? I can't hear my own voice right now.' He raised his arms to simulate the act of playing, picking up an imaginary trumpet. 'Name this tune!' he challenged. Then he formed an embouchure and 'played' 'Happy Birthday' all without aids. His pitch was perfect. 'See? Muscle memory,' he said, and I clapped.

We spoke about synaesthesia and Sean told me how systems fire together when he's playing music. He placed his hands on the table and looked at the ceiling for a moment. 'I want to say it's visual, but it's not, because I've never actually "seen" it. But I do see it visually in my mind.' He explained that when you play a low note on a brass instrument, you have to make an 'ow' sound with your lips. He showed me the action and asked me to try it with him. 'When you play the middle range it's more like an "a" and high range is "e".' I nodded and waited for him to continue. 'I'm not sure how exactly,' he said, 'but I see and feel these things together, you know?'

Sometimes Sean even thinks in a certain key. He pointed to his chest. 'G major has a very different feeling in here. It's a lot more optimistic. A major is just a flirt.' He continued, 'It's just "get out of town, you. Stop it!" E major is a nervous girl. Also, it's different parts of the body. A low G sharp is my right foot; an F natural is my left arm.'

Danny's methods were different. He was irked by the focus placed on vibration. 'People tend to think it's just about that, but it's so much more,' he said. 'Vibration is too simplistic.' Danny moved a hand from his head to his heart. 'It's also here, and here too,' he said. At a presentation he gave at a school in Huddersfield, he told the students: 'My body feels very different playing Bach, or Schumann, or Rachmaninoff. Rachmaninoff feels like a woodpecker.' He formed the sign for 'bird'—index finger and thumb pressed together in the shape of a beak—and pressed it repeatedly onto the opposite palm. He asked the children to copy the action and they pecked their hands excitedly.

'Schumann was a bit of a poet,' he continued. 'Think of a cloud on a castle. Try and picture it in your head while I play it.' His fingers ran over the keys of an upright piano on one side of the stage, and several little heads turned to watch. His body bent into the keys, back arching and contracting as he went. Later, he told me that certain pieces might require different kinds of embodied approaches. In some he might move as though there was 'oil beneath his fingers', or his hands might become 'paintbrushes' or 'hammers' during the act of playing.

Research into deaf musicians shows that their engagements and conceptions of music are deeply idiosyncratic, though one researcher, Robert Fulford, has identified different trends in their engagement styles. Some musicians can be understood to be 'auditory attending' and use residual hearing or amplification through hearing aids or cochlear implants, while others consider vibration and vibrotactile feedback as essential parts of the sensory experience. These musicians sometimes dispense with hearing technology in order to focus on the felt aspects of music. Others might be understood as 'visually attending' relying on the score as well as visual cues and strategies in their music-making and playing.

Flautist Ruth Montgomery uses a combination of these styles in her approach. When she plays, she uses hearing aids and much prefers the analogue variety. Despite being profoundly deaf, she's grateful to hear the flute well enough to enjoy melodies. 'I love the feeling of moving my fingers on the keys, as if I am dancing,' she told me. 'And the tonguing-work happening in sync with my fingers and shaping my ideas.'

Like Danny, Ruth cares very little for vibrations. 'I think reading music is the most important thing,' she said. 'After a few years of teaching, I realise that's what I have passed on to my pupils. They are incredibly good readers of music.' In her early years, Ruth never had sign language and didn't meet other deaf children until she changed schools in her teens. She saw this as a loss and spoke of music as a companion that supported her in this time. 'Despite all the stresses I had,' she said, 'music was like my friend. It was always there for me. It gave me so much self-worth.' As an adult, Ruth now has access to sign and the Deaf community. But during those years at school, she felt that music kept her afloat.

Danny also spoke of music as an emotional outlet and explained the ways he forged a relationship with music during his childhood. 'When I was feeling isolated as a teenager, I had a really strong bond with music. I could be creative; I could express myself.' Sean, too, reflected upon a kind of 'call-and-response' relationship between instrument and person.

'I think what a lot of people forget is that it's not just sound when you play a musical instrument,' he explained. 'It's the fact that you're holding something. It's the fact that it's something that will respond to you if you give it something. If you blow into it, press it, you'll get a sound back. To a deaf child, that will be magnified even more.' For Sean, the responsiveness of instruments was set in opposition to the rest of the hearing world.

Like many deaf children, Sean struggled to acquire spoken language. He couldn't speak at all until he was nine years old. 'You know the song "Twinkle, Twinkle Little Star?"' he asked me. 'I could play that on the trumpet before I could say the words.'

In those years without spoken language, Sean felt that his emotional vocabulary was stunted. 'If you can't tell someone how you feel, then everything is happening only on the inside,' he said. 'You don't know the words "shy, nervous, angry, furious, disappointed, crestfallen". You can't express all these, and music just fills those gaps in for you.' Music was different from the feeling of isolation he experienced in mainstream schooling. 'It wasn't feeling frustrated every day. It wasn't feeling inadequate. It was me and the trumpet in a practice room.'

With all the musicians, and with other members of Music and the Deaf, every conversation was a polemic. Sean often clutched his chest when speaking of people he was fond of, particularly some of his first music teachers to whom he feels deeply grateful. Danny often used the sign for 'love' when speaking about his passion for music. In all of them was a hunger to impart their message. It seemed as though their entire bodies were embroiled in its service, as if each limb conspired to tell me something important. They leaned towards me in a stance that demanded attention. Listen to me, they said. Believe me.

On one of the quieter days, I sat in the office with Danny and one his interpreters who trail him throughout the day. Over coffee we chatted about music and identity politics. Danny explained that he considered himself culturally Deaf. He uses British Sign Language, is an active member of the Deaf community, has a signing Deaf partner; but it's not as simple as that. Sometimes the labels you choose for yourself don't stick. 'I'm really between the two communities,' he clarified. 'Because of the music, I tend to get pushed out.'

I nodded as Danny used his hands to explain this further. He recruited one hand to represent himself: a sole index finger hovering at his chest. The other became a force that acted upon him, pushing him to the margins of the signing space.

Both Deaf and hearing people have struggled with his position. 'But you're musical!' they say. 'A little bit hearing.' He tells them, 'No, I'm profoundly Deaf.' In other circles, he gets into trouble for picking moderately deaf pupils when on judging panels for musical events. 'People will say to me later, "I think we should be encouraging the profoundly deaf child."'

'It's a battlefield,' his interpreter said aloud, signing at the same time. 'You can't win either way.'

Towards the end of my time in the UK, I watched 4ORTE perform at the House of Lords in London. Dressed in formal wear, they played 'Ave Maria' in a grand room before the Thames. Danny addressed the audience, sharing his hopes of raising awareness and expectations about what deaf musicians can achieve.

Ruth Montgomery writes that 'Music is not about hearing any more than language is.' I found myself contemplating this when I spent time in a school for deaf children in Sydney. I watched as students pressed their ears and bodies to speakers and instruments, extracting whatever they could from the experience. I asked them what they thought about music and its place in their lives. One student told me he found music boring and began mocking the affectations of singers, putting a hand to his chest and moving in a way that suggested melodrama and excess. He screwed up his nose and gave a dismissive flick of his wrists. 'I don't like it,' he said.

Upon seeing this, another student shook her head in disbelief. 'If you don't have music, you don't have feeling,' she said. 'Life would be lonely. Music brings enjoyment and excitement. Without it you'd end up cold-hearted, not feeling sadness, love, humour.' I watched on as they became more and more animated. 'No music is like a life in black and white,' another said. 'Music is the colour in the rainbow.'

I was taken aback by the vitriol, and by the noise in the room whenever I sat in on their music lessons. Volume was often a bone of contention, and an ongoing joke between the hearing teacher and the deaf pupils. The room was cacophonous with electric keyboards being played simultaneously, or from music videos streaming through the smartboard and surround speakers at the front of the classroom.

During one class on 'music in advertising', students used iPads and YouTube to source examples of jingles, and the volume was so high that the teacher pleaded with her students. 'Can we please turn everything down? I'm getting a headache!' In response, the Deaf teaching assistant pointed to her ears. 'Better for me than for you!' she said. A student laughed and replied, 'Yeah, we like it loud. Really loud.'

•

Whn attempting to see sound, researchers blast audio frequencies through a surface and watch their effect upon matter. If you play a recording of a chromatic scale into water, formations appear like fractals. Each note leaves a distinct pattern. The science of visualising audio frequencies is called 'cymatics', and researchers use fire, sand and even electricity to map pieces of music and make visible their vibrational energy.

Functional MRIs of the brains of deaf people have shown that *feeling* music stimulates the same part of the brain that is normally used for processing sounds. Cognitive linguists have also found that the left hemisphere regions responsible for tracking music are the same that are active when deaf people communicate in sign.

Historians have speculated that the Deaf might be the only culture without their own music and Deaf Studies scholars have begun correcting the record. Anabel Maler reminds us that the tradition of signed song extends back to at least the early twentieth century and Deaf people create sign language music, grounding that music in the characteristics of sign. Others note the 'Bison Song', a sporting fight song originating from Gallaudet University, which involves arranging signs to certain beats.

Oliver Sacks writes, 'Even profoundly deaf people have innate musicality,' and researchers have observed that deaf babies produce songlike babbling with their hands, creating movements that are rhythmically distinct from those of hearing babies.

I spoke with prominent music educator Christine Rocca about her experiences teaching deaf children over the course of her career.

People used to say she was cruel, forcing children to behave like they were hearing. But for her, including deaf children was a matter of equality. 'I think all have access to music,' she told me. 'It's just how you adapt and differentiate your skills to enable that to happen.' It was her belief that talent and interest was as varied in her students as it is in hearing pupils. Having taught both Danny and Ruth, she stressed the possibilities of giving deaf kids a musical education, especially one that is age-appropriate.

She warned against the soft bigotry of low expectations—against patronising deaf students and assuming a lack of ability. Permanent percussion, she believed, was limiting. 'Who knows the potential of those students?' she mused. A passion for music, she went on to say, is not determined by how well you can hear. 'It's not because you're aural or signing or bilingual. It doesn't sit like that, for me anyway,' she said.

Christine reflected on the Deaf-centric origins of music in the Deaf world. She explained that the very first music programs for the deaf started at Rochester School for the Deaf, a signing school in the United States. 'They had a marching band,' she said. 'And it's brilliant because if you're blowing a clarinet, you're not speaking, and you're not signing. Music *is* your language.'

Every year, when I was a child, my grandfather used to take us kids to the Orange Blossom festival, a country fair held near our home. On the morning of the fair, our street would be full of sightseers, and Grandpa used to bring his video camera to film the vintage cars, the fire brigade, and community groups with their banners. At the front of the parade there was always a marching band complete with bagpipes and big French horns. Grandpa loved to arrive early so he could see them on their lap around the neighbourhood. Since he died, I cannot hear the sound of bagpipes without crumpling. I'm yet to brave the festival without him.

Grandpa had a few memories of music from before he went deaf. There was one song that stayed with him all his life. Between his home in Wallbrook and his first school, there was an orphanage Grandpa used to pass as he walked. One morning, on his way to school, he heard a girl singing to herself. He wasn't sure whether she had made it up on the spot, but recounting it was so upsetting that he couldn't repeat the lyrics aloud. When he tried, his voice buckled. Instead, he wrote them down for me on a piece of scrap paper.

'Where is my mother, down in her grave?

Shall I go and get her up? Feed her from my little cup?

That's enough today. That's enough today.'

•

For most of my adult life I've almost exclusively (and compulsively) dated musicians. Within these relationships, I've been struck by the ways I've listened to music differently from my partners. I tend to focus on melody and lyrics, following the storyline. But many of my boyfriends were fascinated by things that were incidental or secondary to me, like the quality of production or the bass line, the instrumentation. It was only in my early twenties that I realised music-induced goosebumps were not a universal experience. For my grandparents, music had little to do with fine bones and membranes at the side of the head. Instead, the whole body was the membrane.

A few years ago, at a family barbecue, my grandparents and I ended up nestled around my piano. While everyone else was busy with desserts and coffee, I started to play. Nanny edged forward and perched on the lip of the lounge cushion and Grandpa sank deeper into the sofa. After a while, Nanny dragged a chair and sat beside me. She placed her hands, wrinkled and papery, on the keys.

'Your turn!' I told her.

She shook her head but kept her fingers on the ivory. I nodded. 'Go on!' She pressed down and jumped back. 'No, you carry on,' she said, and lay her hands on the wooden body of the piano. She told me she could feel the vibrations.

I played a melancholy song and wondered if my grandparents were privy to it. When I stopped, Nanny turned to me. 'I would love to hear, you know,' she said.

'What would you like to hear?'

'Everything. Everything! The voices of my family, music, your piano and your singing. I really would.' She turned to Grandpa then and asked if he would like to hear music.

'When I started school at five years old,' he said, 'we were listening to the piano and the teacher told me, "Close your eyes, you can hear the music better."' For a moment, he let his head loll back as if savouring the memory. 'That's right, isn't it?

'I remember that,' he said. 'I remember that.'

19.

On the night Grandpa died, I was at the Sydney Opera House, waiting to see a show. I had missed calls from both of my parents, but it was my dad who told me the news. I don't remember what he said, or how he said it, only that time seemed to warp around me.

Grandpa was alone when he went, the family having left the palliative care wing only hours beforehand. Though it plagued us, particularly Mum, who was determined to be there, it seemed fitting that he'd go on his own. He never made a fuss about anything and wasn't about to start.

Though the rest of the grandchildren felt they had said their goodbyes and wanted to remember him as he was, I needed to be there. I rushed from the city, driving out west to the nursing home. With Nanny, my parents, and Ray and Ruth, I stayed at my grandfather's bedside until the undertakers arrived.

In the final days of his life, Grandpa was put on morphine and slipped into a sort of twilight state somewhere between dreams and reality. Once, he awoke, all muddled, and asked for Lawson. Another time he told us the Germans were coming. The things he saw were often absurd, even comical. But most of the drug-induced hallucinations were uncannily lifelike, the cast of characters being drawn from the people and places closest to him.

He told me one day that he'd seen me running around the garden. 'I was trying to catch you,' he said and simulated a chase with his hands. A few hours later he sat up and looked at Nanny. 'I'm ready to go,' he announced, 'but I've got no keys.' He reached for my grandmother then. 'I'm waiting for you,' he said, and drifted back to sleep.

Grandpa's decline had been long and protracted, dragging out over a decade. He disappeared in increments over years—first his energy levels, then his walking, and then his organs, one by one, began to shut down. His life in Australia was marked by the threat and thievery of illness. Within a few years of arriving, Grandpa received a false diagnosis of cancer. At the age of sixty-five he believed himself to be dying. The shadow found on his lungs turned out to be emphysema—a much slower killer—and Grandpa never smoked again. But a decade or so on, the shadow had caught up with him.

By Grandpa's early eighties, he could no longer manage long distances with just a walking stick, and Mum bought the wheelchair. We used it for the first time on a family holiday in New Zealand. Mum and I took turns pushing him around the tourist attractions, struggling to control our speed down hills and around corners. On the day we visited the Wellington Botanic Garden, the pair of us wrestled with the flimsy brakes and the limits of our combined upper body strength, while Grandpa covered his eyes as we went screaming (and swearing) down the steep valleys of the park.

Though chronic illness was a stealthy predator, Grandpa had a remarkable knack for evading its grasp. Even after bouts of pneumonia and cardiac trouble, he kept surprising us, hanging on in spite of himself. One year, when I was in my mid-twenties, my parents went to Europe for four weeks and asked me to stay in the family home to keep an eye on Nanny and Grandpa. In that time, my grandfather developed one of his chest infections. He said he was fed up with life and refused to shower or change out of his pyjamas for ten days. When he stopped eating, I called Ray and Ruth for backup, and they arrived with McDonald's and fish and chips.

At night I stayed up watching TV in my parents' bedroom. Once the lights were off, I could hear, ever so faintly, Grandpa's cough through the wall. Eventually, when threatened with an ambulance, Grandpa eased himself back into the world. The day my mother returned, I almost collapsed into her, grateful that my worst fears had been avoided, but also that I could hand back the reins.

The fact of his decline hung around like static and we wasted no time. Mum organised trips up and down the coast, or into the highlands. Mostly it was just the four of us: Mum, Nanny, Grandpa and me. Between us, we developed an unspoken 'bucket list' and visited Grandpa's favourite places, behaving like tourists even in our own city. We rode the ferries in the harbour and wheeled him around Circular Quay, stopping at each plaque on the Sydney Writers Walk so Grandpa could read the inscriptions and tell us about each of the featured authors.

He had survived so much that my grandfather's final admission to hospital on New Year's Day didn't feel damning at first. We had worried about Grandpa on Christmas Day when he stumbled next door for an afternoon sleep. As I helped him across the back deck, I needed my full strength to shoulder his weight. When I returned, Mum hung her head and speculated that this might be our last Christmas together. But hope is a seductive thing, and for the first weeks of his admission, I dedicated myself to cheerleading his efforts during his physio sessions, where therapists tried to corral him out of bed. 'If you don't get up soon, you won't get up again,' they warned him. At first, I could see the fear in his face. Soon it became fatigue, and finally resignation.

During the five months he spent in hospital, rehab and the nursing home, Mum and Uncle Ray took time off work whenever they could, and us kids filled in the gaps. I was in the final stages of writing my thesis and I often spent my days working next to him on my laptop, interpreting the appointments with the specialists and social workers. A week before the heart attack, I submitted my PhD. I lay a printed copy on Grandpa's bed and he thumbed through it, managing to read a few pages before he fell asleep, his glasses still pinned to his nose.

Before Grandpa died, he told my mother he didn't want a funeral. He wanted to spare us the expense and saw no need for fanfare. We told him where his remains would be kept, in the grounds of a church out in the Hawkesbury region where Nanny and Grandpa had first lived in Australia. Us kids were all christened there. We told him that we'd bought the neighbouring plot for Nanny, and that when her time came, they'd be together.

A few days after he was cremated, my family held a memorial service on the banks of the Hawkesbury River, one of his favourite places. Behind us, the she-oaks that lined the riverfront were bending in the breeze. I read an informal eulogy and we played the music that Grandpa had requested: 'Danny Boy', 'Jerusalem' and 'It's a Long Way to Tipperary'.

•

The first death in any family unit is seismic. All of us felt the hollow of his absence, the incompleteness of birthdays and graduations. Up until then, I'd taken for granted the fullness of our ensemble. There were twelve places at every table we ever set for family dinners. With the births of each great-grandchild, our numbers had expanded over the years but never contracted. The world, though it looked the same, was off kilter.

Grandpa's passing fractured something elemental in our family's framework. In the last hours we had with Grandpa, as we all hovered around him—unsure of where to place ourselves—Mum climbed into her father's bed and lay beside him. She looked so small under the bedclothes, tucked beneath his wing.

In those first days without him, I focused almost exclusively on Mum and Nanny. We sat in a stupor, sipping tea and talking whenever we could manage it. Before then, we had busied ourselves with various tasks. But once Grandpa was gone, there was nothing left to *do*. My mother surrendered to her grief like a building being razed. Her body curved in on itself as if nursing some terrible injury.

Following his cremation, Nanny moved the mahogany box containing Grandpa's ashes around the various rooms of the house. She kept him at first in the bedroom, then on the drinks trolley in the front room, and finally retired him to the spare room where he sat surrounded by the multiple ticking clocks on the dresser. It would be several months before we could bury him at the church.

No longer wracked with anxiety about Grandpa, I began to worry about my grandmother, whose loneliness was punishing. I feared the 'widowhood effect' where mourning spouses are 30 per cent more likely to die within six months of their partner. Nanny remained fit and well, but her behaviour soon became erratic and childlike. She started obsessing over small things, insisting on having reserves of bread and medication, and hoarding cash in the house. On a weekly basis, Mum had to drive her up to the ATM to withdraw funds—$400 each time—to stash in her hiding spot.

Nanny grew increasingly sensitive to being left out. There were occasions where she broke down over what she saw as efforts to exclude her. One time, I visited the house and rushed in to help my sister with my niece, who hadn't slept all night. Nanny saw my car in the driveway, and because I'd failed to greet her first, marched over and demanded an explanation. Another time my sister failed to respond to a text message and Nanny appeared at the door in tears.

There were many times I tried to soothe and console her, offering up affirmations and assurances of love. But my grandmother was unbending and huffy. On occasions Mum was visibly grieving, Nanny was stony. On the first Father's Day without Grandpa, I bought my mother flowers and a card. My grandmother looked slighted. 'It's hard for me all the time,' she wailed.

Next to theirs, my grief felt a small and insignificant thing. I began stifling it, and focused on my romantic relationship at the time, which had begun to fray. Before Grandpa's death, I had stopped sleeping, mulling over the horrors of the ward: the homeless man whose family had abandoned him, the stroke patient who couldn't have been much older than me. Afterwards, my partner confessed his jealousy. My attention and affection had been split, and he had felt secondary. His own father had died a few years before of cancer, and it was difficult to watch my grandfather live to a ripe age—to have the privilege of knowing his grandchildren, his great-grandchildren too.

As a gesture of acknowledgement (or was it repentance?) I tried to make my pain smaller in his company. The loneliness of grief grew thicker as I began hiding it from his view, counting the milestones alone—the one-month mark, the six-month mark. Sometimes it seeped out of me, often at inopportune moments: at traffic lights, or after a night of drinking, and once during a holiday I had booked with money that Grandpa had left me.

For some time, I withdrew from the Deaf community. I stopped going to Deaf events and rarely saw my Deaf friends, though they sent their condolences and texted to check up on me. My retreat was never a conscious one, but anything d/Deaf-related sent an electric current through my chest. I couldn't sign or touch my own research for months.

When my relationship ended, sometime before the first anniversary of Grandpa's death, I was a husk of my former self. I ached for the past and for the future I had planned. The twin losses left me raw. I hibernated in my home, trying to keep sane as the pandemic took full flight.

•

For many months, my grandparents' home felt like a museum of hurts. Grandpa's armchair sat like a wound in the living room, his imprint still left in the cushions. Nanny stopped sitting in hers and moved to the couch that faced the window. Sometimes the TV was on for company, but mostly she sat there watching the cars and bicycles go by, waiting for my parents to return home from work. In the house next door, Turbo did the same, propped on the top of the couch until he heard my mother's tyres on the driveway. Mum would often come home to Turbo waiting at the front door, and Nanny at the back.

Roughly a year after Grandpa died, Mum decided to retire from her job as a principal. She took up casual teaching and spent her days off taking Nanny for high tea and outings to local nurseries. My parents started inviting Nanny over on a regular basis. On Wednesday nights, she joined them for dinner, and every second weekend, Ray and Ruth had Nanny to stay, taking her to the RSL club on a Friday night where she entered meat raffles and played games of trivia with my cousins.

We had expected some changes, but over months, Nanny became more and more scatterbrained. Without my grandfather to remind her, she strained to remember the names of things. There were significant family stories she plain forgot, and she started using memory aids, writing lists and using calendars to help make sense of her days. One afternoon, while having lunch at a local cafe with Mum and Nanny, some old family friends approached us and launched into conversation. Though Nanny had known them well, a glazed expression fell over her face.

Domestic tasks became difficult and tiresome, and Nanny stopped cooking. The shepherd's pies and lemon delicious puddings she used to bake were soon replaced by frozen food she warmed in a portable mini oven. Housekeeping was no longer the habit it had been and began disappearing from my grandmother's routine. For many years, Mum had hired a cleaner to take care of the bigger undertakings like mopping or scrubbing the bathroom. But soon the smaller tasks like washing up began slipping her mind. Tea-stained crockery was placed back in the cupboards, dirty cutlery in the drawers.

On a visit to Ray and Ruth's, Nanny collapsed in the bathroom after an episode of vomiting and pain in her arms. She spent a night in hospital, and we grew concerned about leaving her alone. Shortly afterwards, we moved my grandmother into the family home, and my sister and her two kids moved from the main house into the granny flat.

The process was bittersweet and a whole-family affair. Nanny was enthusiastic about the change, but uneasy about packing her life into boxes. I spent days with Mum and Uncle Ray sorting out my grandparents' belongings, helping Nanny decide what to keep. We went through cupboards of papers and the shelves of books. Nanny stood beside me and pointed to things she wanted taken next door. We made piles for charity and piles for family members to inherit.

Everything my grandparents had ever owned was covered in a thick layer of dust, and we formed a kind of production line, wiping down the items and moving them to their final resting places. My dad and siblings carried Nanny's living room furniture to the main house, and my cousin Ben helped us convert one of the bedrooms into a kitchenette so Nanny could retain some independence and use her own things.

For as long as we could, we put off dismantling my grandfather's DVD collection. We left the job till last, tiptoeing around them. Grandpa's favourites were distributed among us, but most were bundled into plastic bags and laid on the front lawn with the unwanted furniture and knick-knacks. 'It would kill him to see this,' Ray kept repeating. 'I know,' my mother said. 'But we can't hold onto them forever.'

In David Kessler's *Finding Meaning*, he tells an anecdote about First Nations villages in the north of Australia that mark someone's passing by moving a piece of furniture or something else into their front yard. The whole community does so as an act of solidarity, but also as a way of making the loss visible. That way, when the bereaved family wake up, they can see that the world has changed not only for them, but for the people around them.

As I stood with the piles of my grandfather's belongings, I couldn't get that image out of my mind. It felt as though my grief—perhaps all our grief—was suddenly upended on our lawn, and I had no choice but to witness it.

On the first anniversary of his death, I visited the site of Grandpa's ashes with Nanny, Mum, Ray and Ruth. As a kind of commemorative gesture, we poured a beer into the earth and watched it disappear. When his birthday came around, we took my nieces to the park by the Hawkesbury River and ate fish and chips. But on the second anniversary, I decided to go to the cemetery alone. I sat on the grass, which had completely grown over the dirt, and began a kind of reckoning.

It was two years before I turned any real corner in my grief. There were little victories along the way—moments of healing where sorrow gave way to feelings of tenderness. On walks around Sydney's foreshore, I listened to podcasts about mourning, sometimes burning through whole seasons in single sittings, and felt a kinship with guests who shared their stories. There was a frankness to them that felt soothing and validating. Sometimes the episodes triggered memories and I smiled weakly at the odds and ends they surfaced.

After several months away, I began to yearn for Deaf company. I attended Deaf events and as my hands leaped into action, I felt nearer to Grandpa, connected to a part of my heritage. But otherwise, I remained stuck in a kind of vortex. It wasn't until the second anniversary of his death, as I sat in the deserted churchyard, that I thought to address my grandfather directly.

I lifted my hands and began to sign. I imagined Grandpa before me and told him how I'd been hurting. The world was an unrecognisable place, upended in the throes of Covid, and I asked him to send relief—something, anything to restore me. That afternoon, my dearest friend gave birth to a baby boy.

Around the same time, Nanny began to seem more like her buoyant self. Though her mind and memory continued to fade, she regained some of her spark. She wanted to get out and about more often—for coffee or lunch, or to get extra groceries—and always insisted that she pay. As lockdowns lifted, we took her with us to visit friends, cafes and even to a school fete where she bought snow cones and second-hand toys for my nieces.

Getting around is harder for her these days. Her arthritic knee, which she refuses to have surgery for, gives her a lot of pain, and limits the distances she can walk. At the shops, she likes to lean on her trolley for extra support. For longer journeys she's just begun to use Grandpa's wheelchair.

My grandmother's life isn't what it was, but there's a peace to her demeanour. On warm days she sits on the back deck with her bucket hat and wraparound sunglasses. Turbo, who has become her doting companion, sits at her feet while she daydreams or tells whoever's present about Grandpa, often as if we've never met him.

In the second year of the pandemic, when I met my now-fiancé, Nanny was thrilled. When I began bringing him home, Nanny regaled him with endless retellings of her core narrative. 'I was married for sixty years,' she would say, pausing for emphasis. 'We were good friends,' she'd tell him, making the sign for 'friends'—one hand wrapped over the fist of the other, and then moved up and down. 'We could talk about anything.'

Away from my mother's gaze, Nanny sometimes tells me that she's waiting to be with Grandpa again. 'It's just a matter of time,' she says. 'We'll be together soon.'

I ask her to keep waiting, joke that she's not allowed to go anywhere. Not yet.

AFTERWORD

SKSK

In the final months of writing, I took up swimming. It became a kind of meditative practice. When I would glide down the lanes, my body plunging through the water, my mind went quiet, momentarily still. Sometimes, as I counted the laps, I thought of Nanny and the times she used to watch me in the backyard pool, Grandpa hanging over the fence to film my somersaults and dives. On boiling summer days I'd plead with them to join me, but they never accepted the offer. Nanny was always petrified of water, having never been taught to swim, and they both hated getting it in their ears. The changes in pressure could leave them aching for days.

They would watch their Australian grandbabies splashing, bombing and pin-dropping into the deep end, and eye us with bemused affection. We must have looked like seals in the sunlight, our skin laced with sunscreen—slinky, wet and glistening.

Whenever I was underwater, I felt most alive, and the closest to being deaf I can imagine. Beneath the surface, my hearing grew dull. Sounds slackened and were swallowed by the molecules, with only the rhythm of my heartbeat keeping time as I moved. As a child during bathtime, I used to submerge myself and become absorbed by my mother's tapping hand, and the way it became a muted kind of pulse as it thrummed against the sides of the tub. In those moments, I'd feel as though I'd somehow climbed into the space of deafness. Though it was merely a childish imagining— no different to dressing up in their clothes or wearing Nanny's hearing aid—even then, perhaps, I was fumbling around in search of my grandparents.

For much of my adult life, I embarked on a kind of quest, looking for a place I could anchor myself among my grandparents' stories. For many years, the granny flat was the closest thing I could find—a location where I stood at the frontier, crossing back and forth between worlds. Before we took it apart, I hired a professional photographer to document the home as it was. When my sister moved in and renovated it, knocking down walls with a hammer and crowbar, it felt inevitable—like a natural form of growth. Still, it left me reeling. It took me a long time to realise that the space was merely a container for us, for our past.

Now, when I want to remember, I take myself down to the water.

.

Not long ago, I had a dream that we took the whole family out on a boat as a way of marking Grandpa's departure. Somehow, he was still with us, chatting and pointing out the sights as we sailed him around the Sydney heads, passing the cruise liners he loved to film. We travelled down the networks of rivers from Barrenjoey to the Hawkesbury, down the Nepean and then back again to the harbour. At the journey's end, everyone disembarked except for my grandfather. Though nobody spoke, we all knew it was time. We were sending him back to sea. Back to England.

He held both my hands as the ship pulled away from the shore. 'You'll have to visit in the spring,' he said, 'or anytime, really.' I nodded, making him a silent promise. As I began to wake, I could still feel, ever so softly, the texture of his fingers slipping through mine.

REFERENCES

Aristotle, 1967, *Poetics*, Ann Arbor, University of Michigan Press.

Bauman, H.D.L., 2014, 'DeafSpace: An architecture toward a more liveable and sustainable world', in Bauman, H.D.L. and Murray, J. (eds.), *Deaf Gain: Raising the stakes for human diversity*, Minneapolis, University of Minnesota Press, pp. 375–401.

Bauman, H.D.L., 2004, 'Audism: Exploring the metaphysics of oppression', *Journal of Deaf Studies and Deaf Education*, vol. 9, no. 2, pp. 239–245.

Bauman, H.D.L., 2008, 'Listening to phonocentrism with deaf eyes: Derrida's mute philosophy of (sign) language', *Philosophy of Disability*, vol. 9, no. 1, doi: http://commons.pacificu.edu/eip/vol9/iss1/2.

Browning, R., 2004, 'Home Thoughts, from Abroad', *Selected Poems*, London, Penguin Random House.

Cain S., 2013, *Quiet: The power of introverts in a world that can't stop talking*, USA, Crown Publishing Group.

Carty, B., 2011, 'Strong and proud: Deaf community has no need for self-appointed champions', *The Conversation*.

Davis, L.J., 1995, *Enforcing Normalcy: Disability, deafness, and the body*, London, Verso.

Davis, L.J., 1997, 'Constructing normalcy: The bell curve, the novel and the invention of the Disabled body in the nineteenth century', in Davis, L.J. (ed.), *The Disability Studies Reader*, New York, Routledge, pp. 9–28.

DeLaurenti, C.A., 2005, 'On phonography: A response to Michael Rüsenberg', *Soundscape*, vol. 6, no. 2, pp. 6–9.

de Saint Loupe, A., 1996, 'A history of misunderstandings: The history of the deaf,' *Diogenes*, vol. 44, no. 175, pp. 1–25.

Didion, J., 2005, *The Year of Magical Thinking*, New York, Knopf.

Fulford, R.J., 2013, 'Interactive performance for musicians with a hearing impairment', doctoral thesis, Manchester, Manchester Metropolitan University.

Fulford, R., Ginsborg, J. and Goldbart, J., 2011, 'Learning not to listen: the experiences of musicians with hearing impairments,' *Music Education Research*, vol. 13, no. 4, pp. 429–446.

Glennie, E., 2003, 'How to Truly Listen', TED Talk.

Hall, W.C., 2017, 'What you don't know can hurt you: The risk of language deprivation by impairing sign language development in deaf children', *Maternal and Child Health Journal*, vol. 21, no. 5, pp. 961–965.

Hall, M.L., Hall, W.C. and Caselli, N.K., 2019, 'Deaf children need language, not (just) speech', *First Language*, vol. 39, no. 4, pp. 367–395.

Johnston, T., 2006, 'W(h)ither the deaf community? Population, genetics, and the future of Australian sign language', *Sign Language Studies*, vol. 6, no. 2, pp. 137–173.

Johnston, T. and Schembri, A., 2007, *Australian Sign Language (Auslan): An introduction to sign language linguistics*, Cambridge, Cambridge University Press.

Kessler, D., 2019, *Finding Meaning: The sixth stage of grief*, London, Penguin Random House.

Kolb, R., 2013, 'Navigating Deafness in a Hearing World', TED Talk.

Ladd, P. 2005, 'Deafhood: A concept stressing possibilities, not deficits', *Scandinavian Journal of Public Health*, vol. 33, no. 66, pp. 12–17.

Loeffler S., 2014, 'Deaf music: Embodying languages and rhythm', in Bauman, H.D.L. and Murray, J. (eds.), *Deaf Gain: Raising the stakes for human diversity*, Minneapolis, University of Minnesota Press, pp. 436–456.

Maler, A., 2016, 'Musical expression among deaf and hearing song signers', in Howe, B., Jensen-Moulton, S., Lerner, N. and Straus, J. (eds.), *The Oxford Book of Music and Disability Studies*, New York, Oxford University Press, pp. 73–91.

Mirzoeff, N., 1995, *Silent poetry: Deafness, sign and visual culture in modern France*, New Jersey, Princeton University Press.

Montgomery, R., 2005, 'There's no point in teaching deaf children music, is there?' Bachelor of Music dissertation, Cardiff, Royal Welsh College of Music and Drama.

Morgan E., 2021, 'Lost touch: How a year without hugs affects our mental health', *The Guardian*.

Padden C., 2007, 'The decline of Deaf clubs in the US: A treatise on the problem of place', in Bauman, H.D.L. (ed), *Open Your Eyes: Deaf Studies talking*, Minneapolis, University of Minnesota Press.

Sacks, O., 1989, *Seeing Voices: A journey into the world of the deaf*, California, University of California Press.

Shea, G., 2017, *The Language of Light: A history of silent voices*, Newhaven, Yale University Press.

Sinclair, I., 2010, *Hackney, That Rose-Red Empire*, London, Penguin Random House.

Stokoe, W., 1960, 'Sign language structure: An outline of the visual communication systems of the American deaf', reprinted 2005 in *The Journal of Deaf Studies and Deaf Education*, vol. 10, no. 1, pp. 3-37.

Taleporos, G., quoted in in Buckmaster, L., 2017, 'The protest and power of disability activism: "It's not as sexy as gay rights or climate change"', *The Guardian*.

Veditz, G., 1912, *Proceedings of the ninth convention of the National Association of the Deaf and third world's congress of the deaf, 1910*, Philocophus Press, Philadelphia.

Note: I have been unable to verify the publication where John Andrew Holmes' words first appeared, but it is likely to be *Wisdom in Small Doses*, published by the University Publishing Company of the University of Illinois in 1927.

ACKNOWLEDGEMENTS

This book wouldn't have been possible without my grandparents—Melvyn and Phyllis Hunt. I am endlessly grateful for their insight, for their love, and for their entrusting me with their stories. This book is for them. Deepest thanks to my family, especially my mum, for tolerating my nosiness and loving me regardless. This book is equally for you all.

I am hugely indebted to Kelly Fagan for believing in this work, and to the rest of the team at Allen and Unwin—Greer Gamble, Samantha Mansell, Sam Ryan and Sandra Buol—for helping bring it into being. Enormous thanks to my editors, Justin Wolfers, Alice Grundy and Elena Gomez, as well as my sensitivity reader, Jessica White, for their keen eyes and thoughtful suggestions. And thank you to Mika Tabata for the stunning book cover design. I couldn't have conjured a more fitting image for the prose that fills these pages.

I'm also grateful to the members of Music and the Deaf and the staff at Mary Hare School for the Deaf for their generosity and support with my research. Special thanks to Associate Professor Kate Rossmanith and Associate Professor Nicole Matthews for all their guidance in the early stages of this project, and to my friends for their enthusiasm and encouragement. To Emma—thank you for calling when words failed me. To Elizabeth, for being my double and lending your voice. To Davey, for reminding me about Austen. And lastly, to my fiancé, James, for showing me what it is to be truly heard.